Surviving
Motherhood

50 Lessons
from the Heart

BY: CYNTHIA TATUM ROBINSON

Surviving Motherhood - Fifty Lessons from the Heart
Copyright © 2019 by Solid Roc Publishing

For permissions you may email the author at
motherhoodlessonsfromtheheart@gmail.com

ISBN:978-0-578-21909-7

Printed in the USA

Dedication

There was a point in my life when I thought caring for four children and authoring a book would become too much of a daunting task. In fact, it seemed nearly impossible. This was indeed a major undertaking that I could never take full credit for.

I affectionately dedicate this book:

> *to my husband Roc, for his love and dedication to our family,*
>
> *to my children Mikayla, Elijah, Alonna, and Josiah who show me each day what it really means to love and forgive,*
>
> *to my two angel babies who taught me that I had taken the gift of motherhood for granted,*
>
> *to my mother who loves beyond measure and gives without restraint,*
>
> *to my father who has always provided a strong voice and stability for our family,*
>
> *and to every mother who unselfishly invests so much of themselves into the lives of their children.*

Table of Contents

Introduction

Mothers exert a tremendous amount of love and energy. Sometimes we just need to be encouraged and reminded that our hard work and dedication is not in vain. This is my sole intention for writing "Surviving Motherhood - 50 Lessons From the Heart."

Mothers share a unique bond, and our experiences are closely related. We share many of the same joys and challenges as we work to reach a common goal; to raise strong, compassionate sons and daughters. I am convinced that every mother has a powerful story to tell. Life brings us all personal experiences that, if shared, will tremendously impact, and influence the hearts and minds of those we connect with.

As you read this collection of short stories you may laugh, cry, and easily relate to the ups and downs of motherhood. More than anything else, my hope is that every mother will be encouraged to fulfill her mission as she strives to survive motherhood.

Motherhood is Not For the Faint at Heart

The unwelcome sound of my 5:30 am alarm startles me. I fumble around tangled sheets and under jumbled pillows to find my phone, press snooze and catch a few extra moments of much-needed sleep. How in the world is it morning already? I feel as though I just closed my sleep-deprived eyes. The rising sun peeks through my bedroom's twisted shades reminding me that there is no rest for the weary. I lay quietly, rehearsing the day's busy schedule in my mind and drag myself out of bed for what promises to be another eventful day. Indeed, I am reminded, that motherhood is not for the faint at heart.

Regardless of what stage of motherhood you are in, we can all emphatically agree that this is not a life for cowards. Our existence is a mixed bag of hugs and tears, highs and lows, doubts and certainties. It's demanding days filled with planning and improvising, mistakes and success, hurts and forgiveness. And somehow mothers still seem to manage it all.

I admit, there are days, I feel I'm not cut out for this thing called motherhood. There have been nights that I have literally cried myself to sleep wondering if I've failed at what I consider to be one of the most important ministries ever to exist. Being a mother undoubtedly allows us to discover remarkable strengths from deep within. Those strengths cause us to love unconditionally and sacrifice everything to support the little humans we have been entrusted with.

I often ask my mother why she never warned me about the challenges that so powerfully lend themselves to motherhood. She intentionally made it look so easy. Only now am I able to truly understand the many sacrifices she made for the sake of her family. There is no end to my gratitude.

On numerous occasions, I have heard many say that motherhood is a thankless job and, at times, it truly feels that way. There are no plaques, major awards, parades, or galas to celebrate mothers. There are no banquets, tributes, accolades or shiny medals. But when I see the smiles on my children's faces, or the gleam in their eyes, I am reminded that it's going to be ok. Their simple gestures, occasional text and tight hugs cause me to believe I'm doing something right.

When you are drained physically and emotionally, take a deep breath, say a prayer, and remember, you were built for this. You are substantially stronger than you think and created to overcome any challenges that come your way. You are not insignificant, and neither is your position in life. *You are a mother!*

Comparison Is A Killer

During the initial months leading up to the birth of my first child, I read every parenting article I could get my anxious hands on. I was 27 and somewhat uneasy about bringing a child into the world. I truly believed, if only I could hear from other moms and experts, I would be the best mother ever. I was truly mistaken.

When I compared my life to those so-called motherhood authority figures, I felt like such a failure. Other moms around me always appeared to have it together when I seemed to struggle in so many aspects of parenthood. I'd see other moms so flawlessly put together, prancing around in their high-heels and pushing their $500 strollers, with their perfectly behaved and well-dressed children. And there I was just hoping to find time for a shower and make it out of the house before noon. Now, four children later, I understand that comparing myself to other mothers was entirely unhealthy. It can have devastating effects on your life and the way you interact with your children. When you take your eyes off of everyone else, you are then able to focus on who you are and discover your true purpose in life. You can focus on being a better individual and becoming a better mother.

I have learned that every mother struggles in one area or another. Many are just not open to admitting it for fear of being judged. We are often jealous of a well put-together facade of someone else's life, not their reality. Stop comparing yourself to what is often nothing more than a visual hallucination.

Social media is filled with an overabundance of posts showing friends and acquaintances with well-dressed children posing seamlessly for the camera. Everyone's life appears to be so perfect. Perfect smiles. Perfect lifestyles. Perfect relationships. I guarantee you that is not their everyday reality.

Two years ago, my husband and I decided to take a last-minute trip to the beach to celebrate our wedding anniversary. To me there is nothing more beautiful than miles and miles of picturesque coastline and the smell of the ocean waves. Our family of six, two girls and two boys ages 1, 8, 10 and 15, loaded up the car to drive three hours to the nearest shore. We posted this picture on Facebook. We were all smiles! Well, everyone except my husband pulling a red wagon full of beach necessities. I'd like to fill you in on the reality behind this picture we so eagerly posted on social media. What should have been a three-hour trip took four and a half hours thanks to horrible traffic and a screaming baby. Once we finally arrived, it took us 30 minutes to find parking and another 30 minutes to unload the car. By that time, we were all exhausted, but we mustered up enough smiles for a family selfie. You know, in our eyes, things have to look perfect for social media. It took my husband 20 minutes to set up those obnoxious umbrellas that kept falling over, while I spent the first 15 minutes fussing at the kids for swimming too far out into the ocean. I'd tried to be smart and save the family money so I

packed plenty of sandwiches and snacks. Only, the wind was extremely strong that day; so every time we tried to eat we would literally end up with sand in our mouths. Anyone up for a pimento cheese and "sand"wich?

But this story gets worse. My youngest was terrified that he would be devoured by sharks so he never left my side. Instead, he chose to throw food out for the birds that, at this point, decided to hold a foul family reunion next to our feet. We peered up into the sky waiting for the next bird to settle and, to our demise, noticed a gray and cloudy sky. And without even a full moment's notice, it began to storm. I suppose I'd been too busy, packing our wonderful picnic lunch, that I failed to check the weather forecast.

It seemed as if I could see the approaching lifeguard over a mile away, as he made his way toward us - almost in slow motion - extending my anguish and yelling, "Everyone must evacuate the beach. Lightning has been detected. Attention, everyone must, blah blah blah," is all I heard. We packed up our umbrellas, towels, buckets, and ruined food, along with countless seashells the children managed to collect. In the pouring down rain, we scuffled through the  deep sand to make it back to our truck. And just when you thought it could not get any worse, there was a soaked $70 ticket stuck to my husband's windshield for parking illegally. Yeah, we were not happy campers, just drenched and pretty annoyed. What a perfect way to celebrate our anniversary.

As we headed for the hotel, and attempted to put this crazy adventure behind us, I decided to post a few pictures on social media. We were all smiles in every photo. I can almost guarantee that someone saw our post that day and wished they could trade places with us. But our post was not our reality. Just one perfect example of why you should never compare yourself to the lives of others. You never honestly know what's going on behind the scenes. The saying is, "the grass is always greener on the other side" or, in this case, "the sand is always smoother on the other side." After more than a decade of motherhood, I finally learned to stop comparing myself to other moms. I have no desire to be like any other mother than myself. In spite of my imperfections, I have learned to make peace with what works for my family and be confident in who God created me to be, even if every moment is not a picture-perfect day at the beach.

Always Trust Your Instincts

No matter how old your children are, there is most likely an undeniable bond that will connect you forever. Whether your children are infants, toddlers, school age, or have entered the world of adulthood, mothers are created with this innate ability to know when something isn't quite right with their children. Have you ever struggled with whether you should take your sick child to the doctor against the advice of others? "Oh, they'll be ok" they said! "It's probably just a cold," they said! Turns out things were more serious than others predicted. "Oh, a double ear infection, huh? Thanks, Doc!" It's sorely important to be guided by your inner insight.

I can remember trying to hide a pregnancy from my mother who, at that particular time, lived nine hours from me. I'd just taken a pregnancy test, and because I'd previously experienced two miscarriages, I wanted to wait to share the good news. It would be easy, I thought. We hadn't planned to visit with my family for the next few months and since she lived in Ohio, and I in SC, she would never notice my baby bump. I figured I could even disguise the well-known bouts of morning sickness. I had it all planned out. My mother and I are very close, but I felt it was important to keep this pregnancy under wraps. I wanted to protect her feelings if the unthinkable occurred again.

I vividly remember this crazy moment as if it was yesterday. I was leaving work about noon with the intention of grabbing a quick lunch. As soon as I started the engine in my car my cell phone rang. "Gasp!" It was my mother. Now keep in mind, it had only been three days since my husband, and I learned the good news. "Hi, dear. I was just thinking about

14

you," she said. I quickly responded that I was fine and attempted to divert her attention by asking about her day. I knew she was on to me. My mother went on to ask if there was anything on my mind. How could this be? What am I supposed to say? This was unreal. I immediately abandoned my plan of secrecy and instead burst into tears, sharing our news. There is something particularly odd and reassuring that someone else in the world has that type of connection with me.

As a mother, there are days when I truly understand what my children are saying, without them even uttering a word. Sometimes it is the look on their faces and other times just a strong feeling in my heart that something isn't quite adding up. Throughout my days of parenting, I have learned to trust my gut over any advice I'm given. There have been times when I truly missed the mark by not following my instincts. It had life-changing and devastating effects on our family. We plan to share that story in another book one day. Life has indeed taught me to trust my instincts and my inner voice. I am no longer hesitant about asking questions if something just feels wrong.

I genuinely believe intuition is a special gift endowed upon mothers. If you ever feel something is not right, more than likely, you are correct. Trust yourself.

It Is Never Too Late to Pursue Your Passion

Do you remember the goals and ambitions you established in your youth? Did you aspire to own a business? Have dreams of obtaining a degree? Desire to enter the medical field? As mothers, we all have prevailing dreams and aspirations that at some point seemed attainable. But in our selfless roles as mothers, we somehow placed our deepest desires high on a bookshelf; and seemingly out of reach. As the years passed, our dreams remained but began to settle and collect dust. We become so engrossed in being the best mother possible that, at times, we lose sight of who we are and our personal goals. Although our ministry of motherhood is significant and at times demanding, there is no written rule that we must exchange our dreams for motherhood.

After graduating from college, I spent several years working in the field of broadcast journalism as a producer and news reporter. This had been one of my life-long dreams. But after giving birth to my first child, those dreams quickly faded. I replaced my wireless microphone, pen, and paper for diapers, pacifiers, and bottles. I made a tough decision for the sake of my family. No regrets.

Later in life, I was blessed to find a position that allowed me to be close to my children, while combining my passion for writing, working with the media, and communicating with the public. Being a dedicated mother is critical, but so is discovering who you are as an individual. Even as a mother,

16

remember that you are a uniquely gifted individual created with a purpose. Never forget that. The poet Langston Hughes once wrote, "What happens to a dream deferred? Does it dry up like a raisin in the sun?... Or does it explode? Hold fast to dreams, for if dreams die, life is a broken-winged bird that cannot fly."

Many women are completely fulfilled in their roles as mothers, and what a beautiful blessing that is. But if you are a mother who has buried her dreams, maybe it's time to also begin pursuing your passions again. I understand how scary that can be, but the longer you wait, the more challenging it is to resurrect your ambitions. It takes courage, time management, and tenacity, but you owe it to yourself to begin moving forward.

Children Need Your Presence More Than Presents

As parents, we are constantly bombarded with pressure to purchase the most popular and expensive gifts on the market. We are shamelessly guilted into deeper debt by way of an empty promise that our children will be happier and fulfilled; only to discover the gifts we struggle to purchase are out of style in the blink of an eye.

One Christmas, my sister, Angela purchased my then 3-year-old daughter, Mikayla, a pink baby doll stroller. I'll never forget it. The stroller was on clearance and priced at less than $5. To my demise, that doggone bargain stroller was the only gift my daughter wanted to play with. Imagine my dismay after spending hundreds and hundreds of dollars on toys that never saw the light of day. I kept asking her, no, really begging her to play with the high priced toys and electronics we'd bought. But no, she just kept walking back and forth past me pushing this cheap stroller, almost as if she was purposely taunting me.

I have learned that what matters most is not the amount of money parents and grandparents spend on elaborate gifts, but the quality time we devote to our children. Want to make a significant investment in your child? Focus on quality time and attention. Children need you more than the presents that you bring.

If you can afford to purchase overpriced trendy gifts, then I am in no way discouraging that. Just consider that when children grow older, it's not necessarily the presents they will recall. I hate to admit it, but I have forgotten most of the gifts my parents bought me, even those Christmas presents I know they worked so hard to afford. But I can clearly remember my father driving me to school every single morning, even when I know he was exhausted. I will never forget my mother baking the most beautiful Easter Bunny cake to share with my elementary school classmates. Those were priceless moments they never even realized they were creating.

Time is one of the most precious gifts you can offer your children. So whether it's fishing, board games, or a walk in the park, invest quality time in your children. No matter your son or daughter's age, remember, it is the small moments together that matter most. Take a moment to shut your cell phone off, look into your child's eyes, and discover something new together.

You Will Never Be A Perfect Parent

Not too long ago, my husband and I were in a heated discussion with someone who disagreed with the parenting advice we offered. We felt we needed to speak up because, in our opinion, this involved the safety and security of a precious child. As you can imagine, that conversation did not go over too well. At the height of this exchange, and with a stern look, the other parent yelled, "You all are not the perfect parents." While I can still feel the painful emotions of that evening, he was right.

Those words pricked my heart. Our intentions had obviously been mistaken. But the greatest pain from those spoken words was that he did not understand how much I truly worried about being a great mother to my own children. But, as parents, we obviously had not been transparent enough or shared enough of our struggles to be taken seriously. Even in our attempt to love and protect another child, maybe we came across as if we had it all together. Those words resonated with me for a while, and there are days I still hear him in the back of my head. "You are not the perfect parents." It was heartbreaking.

I'm sharing this story because so many of us struggle with not being the perfect parents to our children, but we are afraid to share that with others. We often live our lives behind a mask to cover the struggles, sufferings, and sorrows that often come with motherhood. But sometimes it's ok to be real and allow other parents to know that you struggle, too. Share the crazy times, share the joyous times, share the disappointing times, and share the tough times. Your transparency will help others see that they are not alone. When parents come to me with worries about their children, I will normally share an example of my struggles. It helps others to realize that you are human, too, and that it's ok to NOT be a perfect parent.

Quitting is Not an Option

Dressed in his Sunday's best, my two-year-old Josiah decided he'd had enough. This birthday photo-shoot was meant to capture a beautiful moment with my toddler. After a pretty long struggle for the perfect photo, Josiah just refused to take any more pictures. My normally vivacious son literally sat with his face buried in his hands. I suppose that was his way of saying, "I quit." He'd certainly had enough!

Ever feel like that as a mom? Even if just for a brief second, we all have moments when we want to give up, throw in the towel, and hand in our keys. Although rewarding, motherhood can also be extremely demanding. We consistently give of ourselves mentally, physically, and emotionally; sometimes without a word of thanks. It's easy to become exhausted in every aspect of our lives. Remember, no matter what motherhood brings your way, you've got this, Momma! You are much stronger than you think and created for a purpose. Take a moment, regroup, and remember that this too shall pass. You possess more strength on the inside of you than you will ever realize. Remember your 'why' and search deep inside to discover the power that lies deep within you. Never give up. Quitting is not an option.

Help Your Child Embrace Diversity & Show Love

In a world so filled with hate, I often wonder what kind of world we will leave for our children and the generation to come. Children are born with an affectionate and loving nature. But something happens along the road to adulthood that causes them to develop prejudices and inequitable opinions of others who are different. As mothers, our words and our actions may perpetuate that cycle.

Discrimination and prejudices are often subjects we avoid, because they are such sensitive topics. As protectors of our children, we must make every effort to create a world where every child feels safe. I want my children to show love to everyone they meet. I want them to speak up when they see other children being mistreated and bullied. There are way too many stories of innocent children ending their lives because they feel overwhelmed by the hurt and hate from other children. That's not ok. Teach your children to speak up for those who have no voice, even if it means just telling a trusted adult. We look to our local schools to create policies to combat bullying. Indeed, those guidelines should exist, however, parents have a significant responsibility to teach this within their own households.

Our children look to us for guidance and direction. So what is the best way to make a difference in our own home? Intentionally speak out against hate and the mistreatment of anyone for any reason. Teach them to embrace diversity by surrounding them with friends who may not necessarily look the way they do or fit into the same financial bracket as your family. This may cause you to step out of your comfort zone, but it is important to educate children about racial and cultural diversity before the world does. A simple way to accomplish this, when children are young, is to purchase books and toys that promote diversity. I recently bought a number of dolls for my niece, Mariah, and I intentionally sought out to find a variety of races and shades of color. This sets a tone of acceptance early on in life.

Mothers should teach children to demonstrate love to the world around them. Our appearances may be different, our learning abilities may be different, our physical make-up may be different, and our backgrounds may be different. We may even have opposite beliefs and opinions. But we are all created on purpose, for a purpose, and we all bleed the same color. Don't shy away from diversity. Embrace it. Teaching your child about kindness and respect starts with you.

Cherish Every Moment

One of the most beautiful moments of motherhood is experiencing those 'firsts' that every parent dreams of. The first time they say, "Mama," begin to crawl or take their first little steps, our hearts are full. With my first three children I could barely wait to experience those 'first' moments with each of them. I would check one milestone off of the chart in anticipation of the next, and the next, and then the next. But something happened I wasn't quite expecting. They were growing up right before my very eyes. Where had the time gone? I was so busy celebrating milestones that I forgot to celebrate every moment in between. In my haste and excitement, I realized that I was rushing away precious moments and priceless memories. Now, with my last child, I have learned to slow down and enjoy every single second of his life. I no longer simply celebrate each milestone; I embrace and celebrate the journey. Maybe because this time around I'm an older mom. I'm in my early 40's with a toddler so I have much more wisdom now than I did when I first became a mom about 17 years ago.

Do you remember when you were a child and someone would ask how old you were? If you were like me, your response would be something like, "11 going on 12." I was young, and there was a sense of urgency in growing up. Now I wish I possessed the power to make time stand still, because, let's face it, life is moving faster than the speed of light.

Embrace their childhood and every stage of life they are in; even the phases of life you may not be so fond of, like middle school! One day you wake up and it hits you, "where did the time go?" My oldest daughter will soon enter college. It seems like yesterday I was impatiently anticipating her grand entrance into the world. Now my heart can barely stand that she will soon be out on her own. So listen mamas, don't rush your child through life. Every single second is significant. Cherish every moment.

Sometimes It's Better Not to Protect Your Children

More than anything, we want to protect our children and shield them from the pain that life often brings. Unfortunately, we will all experience a time when we have to sit back and allow life to educate our children in a way that our words are unable to.

Christmas is always a joyous time for our family. For us, we celebrate what we believe to be the true meaning of 'Christ'mas, and experience fun times baking, shopping, and most importantly, giving to others. However, the Christmas of 2016 was a traumatic time for our family. Just a few days before December 25th, we got a call that my father's brother, my uncle, had been hospitalized. We changed our plans, loaded up the kids and drove about four hours to make sure our Uncle Houston Roberson was ok. What we were hoping would be a short hospital stay turned tragic. Just a few days later Houston was gone.

He was a great man who had influenced many lives across the world. Houston was an academician and a professor at Sewanee- The University of the South. He spent much of his life breaking down racial barriers and making waves in the field of education. His death was heartbreaking to everyone in our extended family and those who knew him well. As you can imagine, the holidays were very different for all of us that year. It was a moment our children will never forget.

I wanted so much to shield them from the hurt and pain death brings. The children continuously begged to visit Houston's hospital room, but I encouraged them to remain in the waiting area for fear his last moments would be too much for their little hearts to handle. My husband kept encouraging me to yield to their request and I reluctantly agreed. That day my children experienced the reality of mortality. We all want to shield our children from pain and suffering but I learned it's not always in their best interest.

You see, as painful as Houston's death was, that day our children gained a deeper appreciation for living. They saw just how quickly life can slip away and why they should never take life for granted. Our children learned to express love every moment possible because every breath could be their last. The countless stories friends told of Houston's time on earth, allowed my children to reflect upon their own lives and consider how they were making a difference in the world. From the perspective of motherhood, I learned that sometimes it's acceptable not to protect your children. Life's greatest lessons are often revealed during life's toughest moments.

Self Love is
A Great Love

From day one I was determined to teach my children how beautiful and handsome they were. I wanted them to understand they never had to measure up to anyone else's standards. They needed to know that the beauty on the inside of them is truly what mattered most. Despite my efforts, I felt like it was me versus the world. My words were canceled out by the Photoshopped images on television and in magazines, teaching my children that they weren't good enough. The images displayed are of females and even males with figures unattainable by most people.

Pressure to look the part, in selfies and on social media, leaves our children in quite a predicament. Can a young person even take a photo without a filter? When my children were younger, they never worried about how others viewed them. But somewhere along the way, that inner confidence was replaced by pressure to meet the world's standards of beauty.

This, too, was a serious issue I dealt with growing up. My weight has always fluctuated, and I've probably experimented with every diet known to mankind. If there were an award for the slowest metabolism in the world, I truly believe I would win the grand prize. No, seriously, I look at chocolate and gain weight. In some ways, I believe my struggles and dissatisfaction with my weight trickled down to my children and helped perpetuate a negative body image for them. In my quest to teach them why they should love themselves, I learned that I was never truly satisfied with my appearance. The little comments I made about my weight and shape, in front of them, inadvertently caused my children to question their appearances. What has this taught me? In order to teach self-love, we must first love ourselves.

Growing up, my oldest daughter had a difficult time accepting the fact that her hair was not as long and straight like her friends. As her mother, I thought she was beautiful with her puffy, curly hair, but she thought otherwise. Every week, it seemed, she would beg for extensions. We worked on loving who she was created to be and put a major focus on the beauty within her. I never wanted her to grow up thinking she had to change her appearance to fit in or to be loved by others.

Parents must also offer their children words of affirmation. Praise them not only for their appearance, but also for acts of kindness and compassion. Focusing on positive character traits reinforces in them that life is much more than looks. We are to help them uncover their strengths and discover powerful ways to use them.

Also, remember the importance of personal contact. I am not the most affectionate person in the world, because that's just not how I am wired. But I always make an effort to hug and kiss my children, to hold their hands, to rub their sweet faces, to give my son a fist-bump, to give them high-fives – anything to show them they are loved. Studies show that skin-to-skin contact between infants and mothers can have astounding results. Quality time and affection from parents is tied to stronger self-esteem and healthier relationships.

Once your children are older, remember that the journey to self-love is not complete. It is an endless battle. Mothers, never stop encouraging your children to love who they are.

Continue to seek ways to make them feel loved and provide strong words of affirmation. Help them realize that they are enough and that they are truly worthy of love.

Pray With Your Children

My husband and I have always vowed to lay a strong spiritual foundation for our children. Part of that foundation embraces the importance of having a consistent prayer life. We believe that prayer causes us to build a stronger relationship with God and helps us release the burdens of our hearts.

We often pray with our children as they head to school or at the end of the day; but one particular night I decided to ask my youngest daughter, Alonna, to say a prayer. So there I sat, on the edge of her bed, placing her little hands inside of mine. Hearing her sweet voice express her gratefulness and anxiety to God truly changed my life. Her prayer was short but powerful. "Thank you Lord for having such a good attitude toward us and giving us what we don't deserve." I will never forget those precious words.

She went on to thank God for her family and ended by asking God to keep her safe from all of the bad people in the world. That night I realized that I was not only teaching her the importance of prayer, but I now had a flawless glimpse into her little heart and mind. Until that night, I never even realized that she was worried about the so-called "bad" people in the world. This prayer made way for a conversation where I learned that her choice of words described the anxiety she felt over the recent violence in our nation. I never realized that current events caused her to fear for her safety. This allowed me another opportunity, as a mom, to reassure her and comfort her in an area that was obviously lacking. I was grateful that she prayed openly that night and it became more of a tradition for us.

From that moment on, I realized that we should not only pray for our children, but also with them. Allow them to pour out their little hearts and minds before God, and before us, so we may better understand their worries. Sometimes it is difficult to encourage our sons and daughters to communicate with us, especially as they grow older. But hearing our children pray openly before God allows us to uncover the matters of their hearts, often without them even realizing it. If you have never prayed with your children, it is not too late to begin. Praying with our children is a wonderful relationship builder, not only with God but also with one another.

There is No Room for Judgment in Motherhood

If there is one thing I have learned about mothers, it is that we are entirely too judgmental of each other. I willingly admit that I have been guilty of judging and sizing up other mothers over the years. The older I have become, the more I realize that most mothers are not in need of judgment, they are in need of support and encouragement. Mothers need to hear someone else say, "I know being a mother is not always easy, but you're doing an amazing job." Instead of offering unsolicited advice or critical comments, offer a hug.

Why are we so critical of each other? Why do we sit in judgment of the way other moms raise their children? Why do we feel the need to constantly criticize mothers who are oftentimes struggling as much as we are? Critical and judgmental attitudes very often expose our insecurities related to motherhood. Let your baby cry it out! Never let your baby cry! Breastfeeding is the only option! Breastfeeding mothers are extremists! People who vaccinate are senseless! People who don't vaccinate are irrational! Home-school! Public School! Natural Birth! C-Sections! The list goes on and on.

If you take a moment to scroll through a few motherhood support groups on social media, you will quickly notice the judgment other mothers give. It is unreal how a simple post about changing a diaper can turn into a debate over cloth or disposables and somehow even turns into a political debate. Have you ever thought about how much easier parenting would be if mothers united to support one another? If we could peer into each other's hearts, we would see that deep down inside, the majority of us are timid, frightened women with a common and indescribable love for our children. We are mothers who only want what's best for our sons and daughters.

My husband and I will occasionally dine out without our children. For some odd reason we, almost always, end up being seated near a couple with young children. Most of the time the mom is painfully struggling to keep her children quiet and often will apologize to us for the extra noise. Although I may prefer a quiet night out with my husband, I make it my mission to ease the mom's worries. Once she hears that we have four children and aren't bothered by the noise, I instantly see a sigh of relief on her face. How dare I stand in judgment of another mother? Who knows the daily struggles she endures or the amount of pressure in her life? It's challenging enough to raise a child but to do that under the scrutiny and judgment of other mothers is preposterous.

Instead of being judgmental, be compassionate and understanding. I challenge you to go out of your way to compliment other mothers. You know how tough life can be! Encourage a young mom who may feel like she's at her wits end. Write a note to a mother who may be drained trying to figure out the teenage years. Send flowers to a mamma experiencing empty nest syndrome. Take time to call the mother of an adult child who may be experiencing loneliness. No matter where you are in your journey of motherhood there is nothing encouraging about being judged and criticized by a fellow mother. Although our lives may be different, we are connected through the bond and association of motherhood. Let's link-up, unite, and create a better world for each other.

Don't Get Caught Without an Oxygen Mask

Here is a multiple-choice question for you. Do you ever feel:

A. Overworked?
B. Overwhelmed?
C. Unappreciated?
D. All of the above?

If your answer is "D," you are not alone! Motherhood is undeniably exhausting. Each day your focus is on placing the needs of someone else before your own. From the moment you open your eyes, until the moment you fall asleep, those little people are at the forefront of your mind. Despite the love we possess for our children, it is easy to become mentally and physically exhausted from giving so much of yourself all of the time.

To effectively care for someone else, we must promote physical, spiritual, and mental care for ourselves. What are we advised to do if cabin pressure drops while in an aircraft? Place the oxygen mask on yourself first and then care for infants and children traveling with you. Raise your hand if you have been caught caring for someone else, without first caring for yourself. I am guilty as charged. Mothers have a natural tendency to place others needs above their own.

Not too long ago I'd completed a hectic day at work, walked in the door to begin dinner and help with homework. I was so tired that my head was spinning, but the dishes were not going to wash themselves. You've been there, right? Well as soon as I decided to rest for the evening, I heard my then one-year-old begin to cry. I jumped up to change his diaper and the next thing I know my husband was picking me up off of the floor. I was out of it and ended up in the emergency room that evening. My children were panicking, my husband was worried, and I was in the hospital concerned about my children not going to bed on time. Doctors completed a C-scan and ran various tests that never pinpointed a physical ailment. The doctor's advice was to rest and find ways to reduce stress. Although I was still partially out of it, I remember thinking, "Does this doctor understand that I have four children?" Of course, I still went to work the next morning. Who has time to rest?

Self-care has been an incredibly difficult lesson for me to learn. Although my work inside and outside the home is quite demanding, it's something I enjoy and appreciate. I am the type of mother who feels guilty for visiting the salon, because I could be washing clothes or hanging out with the children. When we go on vacation, I refuse to just sit and enjoy the scenery of a road trip. I take advantage of the ride, pull out my laptop and complete a project for work. Not because I have to, but because I feel like there are just not enough hours in the day to complete every task. I have been accused of becoming overly consumed by any project or responsibility I take on. There must be a healthy balance.

Please take time for yourself. Read a good book (not work related), take a walk alone, visit a salon (without feeling guilty), journal your blessings, connect with your spouse, pray and meditate. These are just a few examples of ways you can relax and reduce the stress in your life. Eating healthier and exercising is such a huge part of that. I am guilty of buying my children healthy and organic foods, but feeding myself anything I can grab in between meetings, scheduled appointments, and errands. In many ways, turning a blind eye to self-care is extremely selfish because your family needs you to be healthy and strong.

Listen up mothers; don't get caught without your oxygen masks on. Take a deep breath and realize that life will go on even if you take 30 minutes to care for yourself.

Get to Know Your Child's Passion

As a first-time parent, I signed my daughter up for every activity I could find. Mikayla took swimming lessons before she was able to walk. Throughout the years she explored dance, gymnastics, piano, chorus, band, and even sports. I wanted to give her every opportunity I could, no matter the sacrifice. Thankfully, my husband was always on board with the next adventure.

I soon discovered that helping children uncover their passion does not always involve organized sports or activities that cost thousands of dollars. It does involve a commitment of time and attentiveness. Watch your children closely. What causes them the most excitement? What makes them tick? What will they do without you having to beg them?

From painting, to playing sports with friends, building a volcano, catching fireflies, or helping out in the kitchen, allow your children to explore and enjoy the goodness life brings. You will eventually begin to notice the one thing they continue to gravitate to over and over again. More than likely, that's their passion. Begin to nurture that passion by helping them develop the skills to become better. For my oldest, it was singing. Music has become Mikayla's passion and no matter what career she chooses in life, I am quite confident that music will be a big part of that. I never have to force her to sing at home, I never have to force her to listen to music. This just comes naturally.

At times, passion can be indisputable, but other times it takes a little more digging and guess work. If it seems your child has no passion yet, do not give up on them. Continue to introduce new ideas and activities. The Internet and even the library are great sources for that. Often, parents want to push their children to follow in their footsteps or become the person they failed to become. This is a huge mistake that you will both grow to regret.

It's been said to choose a career you love, and you will never work a day in your life. Helping your children discover their passion is significant and vital to their success. Allow your sons and daughters to think outside the box. Maybe they aren't meant to work a 9-5. Perhaps they aren't called to lead a Fortune 500 company. Without passion, a person, young or old will have no direction or true purpose in life. There are no limits for those who realize and develop their passion. It has the power to catapult them into the next dimension.

Sometimes You Have to Press the Reset Button

Have you ever looked back on your life as a mother and considered all of the mistakes you've made? We all have those crazy moments we regret and wish we had the opportunity to redo. Instead of becoming disappointed in yourself, just press the reset button.

The times you've yelled when you should have shown patience... The times you have chosen work over spending quality time with your family... The times you have taken a stressful day out on your innocent child.... Just press the reset button.

Pressing the reset button means forgiving yourself. It means believing that tomorrow is a new day for second chances. Pressing the reset button means showing yourself the same mercy and kindness that you show others. Pressing the reset button means admitting your failures and trusting yourself enough to start over.

After my children are in bed for the evening, I normally take time to replay the events of the day in my head. As much as I know I love my children there are truly times that I feel like the biggest failure among all existing mothers. It is then that I press the reset button by reminding myself that mothers are human too. I press the reset button by reminding myself of the unshakable love I have for my family. I press the reset button by admitting my mistakes to my children. Even on nights when my spirit is broken because of something I have missed, something I have said or something I have done, I press the reset button because everyone deserves a do-over, even mothers.

Pat Yourself on the Back

As amazing as motherhood is, our life is often filled with draining days and maddening moments. We feel as if we are pulled in every direction, juggling numerous never-ending tasks, all while pouring so much into these little human beings who rely on us every waking moment. Don't misunderstand, there are days, well maybe some moments, where I feel like a real pro. Everything seems to be running like a fine-oiled machine. I get everyone to school on time, the house is clean, dinner is prepped and everyone is content, including my spouse. But those moments are oftentimes overshadowed by days when I feel everything is a complete disaster. Yes, even as a mom of four, at times, I wonder if I am doing everything wrong. We all have those moments. And while I certainly cannot speak for every mother, I truly believe we are our own worst critiques.

I am constantly evaluating myself, and God forbid if anything goes wrong, I beat myself up mercilessly. What could I have done differently? Why didn't I think ahead? Why didn't I pack this? How could I have forgotten this? Why did I ever say that? Have I ruined my child's life forever?! I literally drove my child, Josiah, to preschool the other day, began unbuckling the straps of his car seat and realized that he had no shoes on. They were not in the backseat. Nope, his shoes were not in his back pack. They weren't even in the trunk. I'd somehow managed to get him dressed, fed, and into the car without noticing that he was without shoes! I was too embarrassed to even go inside and explain. Every nearby store that sells shoes hadn't opened yet, so I ended up going all the way back home. I'm thinking, "Is there any other mother in the world this scatterbrained?"

In the midst of those crazy, unplanned moments, it is so easy to overlook the ways in which you are making a positive impact on your family. You give of yourself each day and sacrifice beyond belief, but rarely take time to pat yourself on the back.

You encourage your children, your spouse, your friends, and your family but do you ever take the time to encourage yourself? It's just in a mothers DNA to shine the spotlight on everyone else rather than themselves. But consider this, constantly focusing on the negative will literally drain you until there is nothing left. It can easily cause you to slip into depression and trigger feelings of hopelessness. And why beat yourself up, when others will gladly do that for you? Sure, we miss the mark at times but we know deep down inside there are days when we pass those daily motherhood exams with flying colors. Who else can survive on two hours of sleep and still keep the family on its toes?

Even if no one else tells you, you are awesome! Not because you always get it right, but because you survive the crazy challenges and outrageous obstacles that motherhood brings, and you are bold enough to face that challenge every single day.

You Will Reap What You Sow

My parents often tell a story about a very precious, yet strong-willed child. Growing up, this particular middle child was confident, headstrong, and uncompromising. After much prayer and mounds of experimental strategies, my parents headed to the nearest store to purchase a well-known book on raising a strong-willed child. While I'm not too sure if that helped them much, I hear this story very often, of course, because it's a story about me. As you may imagine, my parents receive much joy while telling these stories in front of my children and my children absolutely LOVE hearing them. They find it hilarious that their mother was never a perfect angel.

Their favorite story to tell is about the day I decided I would run away from home. Being the kind and thoughtful child that I was, I wrote my parents a note explaining why I was leaving and where I was going. That was pretty considerate, right? I explained that when they learned how to act, they would know where to find me. I left the complete address, packed my bag and went four houses up the street to move in with a friend. What in the world was I thinking? Sure, it's a pretty comical story now, but as a mother of four, I now feel like I am getting a taste of my own medicine.

Have you ever noticed that the qualities that irritate you most about your children are the ones that remind you of yourself? Seeing yourself in your children can be quite mind-boggling. One moment you are bothered by the way they are

45

behaving, and suddenly you have flashbacks of your own childhood. Maybe it's God's way of keeping us humble!

As a mother, I love to see my son Elijah writing, because putting pen to paper, or in my case, fingers to keyboard, is something I truly enjoy. It warms my heart to hear my daughters sing because music has always been a real passion of mine. I'd love to think that somewhere along the line, I've positively influenced them. I believe that my children are a wonderful combination of my husband and me. What's tough is that they possess our best characteristics as well as those qualities we would rather not discuss. Stubbornness, procrastination, and impatience - I admit it's in our DNA. Empathy for others, confidence, and determination – that's in our family's genetic make-up. Unfortunately, we must take the good with the bad.

Seek to recognize your child's positive qualities and consistently provide positive reinforcement when they make the right choices. When dealing with negative behaviors, especially those you have dealt with first-hand, it's best to vocalize your own struggles and how you overcame them. Don't be embarrassed to admit areas you are still in the process of overcoming. It makes you more accountable and helps your child see that, regardless of age, we should continue to evolve and desire to become better human beings. Mothers are no exception.

Miscarriage is Life-Changing

The death of a child at any stage is a tragedy no mother should ever have to endure. No words adequately describe the pain and emptiness losing a child brings. Although I am blessed with four living children, I am also the mother of two precious angels. So many mothers, like myself, have experienced the pain and devastation of miscarriage. Although statistics show that 25% of women will miscarry, it is often a topic many shy away from. I want to delve a little deeper into this topic to express how miscarriages affect women and the best ways to offer support to mothers suffering from this hardship. This will be one of the longest chapters in this book. But before I continue, I would first like to share two of my blog posts from 2013. They were written only days after learning that I miscarried.

Blog Post March 2013

I've been writing in some form for the past 35 years. I've always been drawn to the combination of words and ink. To me, writing is easier than speaking. Writing is therapeutic. Writing is healing. I'm praying that in some way I am healing...even as I write this. It was only about 4 weeks ago that I decided to blog about the excitement my husband and I felt once finding out we were having a fourth child. I was so excited I could hardly type. Now, my hands also shake as I press the keys on this computer, consequently, for a different reason. Happiness has quickly turned to hurt; pleasure has suddenly become pain, delight...swiftly replaced with distress and disappointment. Utter disappointment. We learned this week that I had experienced a miscarriage. "No, you must be mistaken!" I thought to myself, after not one but three unfavorable ultrasounds. We kept asking for additional ultrasounds because we could not wrap our minds around the fact that our baby, although tiny and barely visible to the human eye.....no longer had a heartbeat. Every time I close my eyes all I see is the dismal black and white picture normally sent home with overjoyed expectant parents....only mine stapled to a doctor's report. All I hear is the static sound....where there should have been a rapidly racing fetal heartbeat. After the ultrasound, my husband and I sat patiently in the waiting room. Praying, hoping, believing God for a miracle. We didn't say much to each other. The silence was awkward. Maybe, just maybe something would change.

The 10 minutes we waited to see the doctor seemed like an eternity. Dr. Carol Ketchen, quietly entered the room, softly closing the door behind her. I could see it in her eyes. I could see it in her eyes. I could see it in her eyes. I knew what she was about to say, but I did not want to hear it. I smiled at her as long as I could in an attempt to keep the tears from rolling. All the while still praying deep down inside that as she opened her mouth...the words she was to utter, would somehow change. They did not.

We'd already picked out a name. Tatum Alexander if we were having a boy and Tatum Alexandria if we were blessed with a girl. My husband really wanted another son. We joked about it, but I knew deep down inside...it really didn't matter to either of us. We were just blessed to be parents again....to be entrusted with four of God's angels. One might think we should have just been happy with three children. In fact, it was difficult for many to believe that this fourth child was not a surprise. Our precious baby was not a surprise...but this heartache was indeed. Why I never got to feel his tiny hand grip my finger, I may never understand. Why I was never allowed to smell the sweet aroma of my newborn freshly bathed...I may never know. Why I was never allowed to gently rub the soft spot in his head or hold him close enough so he could relax to the sound of my heartbeat....I cannot comprehend. God only knows the loss I feel...even after just carrying for 10 weeks. Even in that short time, I'd already fallen in love. There was room in my heart for this child and now my heart is broken. Even with three other children, I love dearly, my heart is broken. My husband's heart is broken. Our three babies are trying so hard to understand why the baby did not keep growing. My six-year-old son, Elijah, looked at me with his bright, glassy, teary eyes and said, "Maybe you're just not eating enough. The baby gets his food from you, so maybe you just need to eat more, and it will keep growing." I regret I told them so early...causing them to endure such unneeded hurt and anguish.

I only hope that one day I will be able to minister to someone who may be going through a similar situation. It is challenging as a leader in the ministry to endure this type of tragedy. Yes, tragedy. I have to constantly remind myself to trust God and know that all things work together for the good of them who love the Lord and who are the called according to His purpose. (Romans 8:28) My husband and I, though we hurt deeply, will eventually bounce back, face the crowds and move on with our lives. But at this moment, I blink to clear the tears from my eyes, in order to see this screen. Right now, I have many regrets....many questions...many uncertainties. I'm hurting as though I've lost a member of my family that I've known my entire life. I cannot explain this grief ...this anguish...and I doubt many would even understand unless *they've been there. I felt as though we'd already bonded. As though he already loved me. As though he couldn't wait to meet me, too.*

As I compose this blog, filled with heartache, grief, and disappointment, I am crushed that I no longer need that two-liter of ginger-ale and the saltine crackers to ease my nauseous stomach. Although, I'm still quite nauseated....only for a different reason. I'm not writing this blog for sympathy. I'm writing this to begin a healing process that I know may take some time. This is indeed much more information than I'd planned to share....only I can't stop writing. I can't stop thinking. I can't stop wondering. I can't stop attempting to understand why a God who loves us so much, a God we serve so faithfully would allow this tragedy to transpire. But in the midst of it all, I will continue to bless God. In the midst of it all, I will continue to put my trust in the One who created me, and the unborn child I never officially met. In the midst of it all, I will find the strength to praise through the pain. Yes, I will. I have no choice. It may take me a while to bounce back, but I have three babies and a husband depending on me...so I must.

Right now, I am just praying for the peace of God that surpasses all understanding. (Philippians 4:7) I rarely get to a point where I just don't feel like praying. I'm there. But I pray anyway, uttering a few words to my Heavenly Father asking for strength. I rarely get to a point where I don't feel like singing. I'm there. But I sing anyway. Occasionally, breaking the silence of sadness in my home, I muster up just enough to sing a few lines.... then the silence returns. But still...I sang. I rarely get to a point where I don't feel like talking to anyone. I'm there. I don't know what to say without crying....and I'm not really the emotional type. As horrible as these last few days have been, it will take much more than this to keep me from giving up on God. I will continue to sing in the silence and praise through the pain. I know that the Holy Spirit, our comforter, is the only one who can replace the emptiness we feel. And though it was only for a short time...I hope I was the best mother I could have been, even to my unborn baby. I will love him forever.

Blog Post April 2013

Exactly one week ago today my life changed forever. That's when I first learned that my pregnancy was not progressing the way it should. Because I've had three perfectly healthy pregnancies, I've never known too much about miscarriages or the emotional roller coaster that would soon follow. Not one day has passed that I have not shed tears, not questioned what I did wrong, and not wondered if there was something I could have done differently. Was it the one day I forgot to take my prenatal vitamins? Should I have rested more instead of going from work, to the grocery store, to rehearsal, then rushing home to cook, clean and check homework? Did I allow myself to stress too much, causing my body to miscarry? I may never know. But in the midst of the questions and in the midst of the pain, I have managed to pray a little longer and sing a little stronger.

One thing I have learned in this past week is that I am not alone in this struggle. I've heard from so many women who have experienced the same heartbreak and anguish connected with miscarriage. I really appreciate those who have inboxed me their stories and those who have prayed for my family and me. This is indeed one of the greatest heartbreaks I have ever experienced. I had no idea that having a miscarriage hurt so bad....not only physically, but mentally and emotionally. I have finally begun to sleep better at night, but every morning I open my eyes, I relive the entire experience, and the emptiness is intensified.

51

During this time my husband has not left my side. He has cried with me, prayed with me and prayed for me. My children are spending their Spring Break in Cleveland with my family so that my husband and I could begin the healing process. I know we will come out of this stronger and wiser. I truly thank God for everyone who has prayed and offered words of encouragement. Soon, I will attempt to begin blogging about something a little more enjoyable to read...but right now I can't seem to think about anything else. In this particular area, I've not grown strong enough to redirect my thoughts, but I'm getting there. I know that I must give this hurt to God and move on with my life. But even when I return to the normalcy of life, I know I will never be the same because I will never ever forget... the angel I carried but never met.

These blog posts express the raw emotions that seemed to consume every fiber of my being. My husband and I had never been so broken. We'd decided we wanted a fourth child. I'd had three fairly healthy pregnancies and never really considered that losing a child to miscarriage was even a real possibility. I now know that I had taken for granted the ability to get pregnant and carry a baby to full-term.

When I found out that our fourth child's heartbeat was no longer beating, I felt hopeless and empty. I'd never even had an in-depth conversation with anyone who'd experienced a miscarriage before so I had no clue what to expect. I was given the option to wait and allow our baby to pass on its own or have a surgical procedure known as a D & C. We chose the latter of the two.

When I went to the hospital, I was taken to the labor and delivery floor. While being prepped for surgery, I could clearly hear the sound of newborns crying in the rooms next to us. Following the short procedure, it seemed as if I barely had time to gather my thoughts. I was whisked out of the hospital within a few hours. My husband and I were crushed. Instead of leaving the hospital, that day, with a bundle of joy, we left with only heavy hearts and unimaginable pain.

When you have a D & C, your body thinks that you've given birth. So I was told to take it easy for a few days. But recovering from the surgery was not the major adjustment. No one explained the emotional toll that would follow the days, weeks, months and years ahead. I'd never felt so empty inside. I'd never cried so much. I'd never felt so lonely. Why lonely? Miscarriage is, in many ways, taboo. People are afraid to talk about it. Many who knew us would speak and act as if nothing ever happened. It offended me, at first, that no one would even acknowledge what had taken place. But later on I realized, most people had no clue what to say, so they didn't say anything. Others who attempted to acknowledge it always seemed to say the wrong things. "Well, at least you have other children." Really? I would think to myself, "Well you have several children, which one of yours would you like to give up?" If only I could have formed my lips to say, "Having other children does not make up for the one I lost."

I am a believer in God, but it pierced my heart to hear people say, "God knows best." I cringed when I'd hear, "It must have been in God's will," or "God needed another rose." Do you know what I wanted? A hug. I needed someone to say they were praying for me without going off on a spiritual tangent. I needed help with my children because I could barely drag myself out of bed. I held it together in front of them, but they knew mommy was different. I needed meals to feed my family who always depended on me to prepare dinner. Through this experience I learned that most people have no clue how to help someone who has lost a child because people rarely talk about it. Grieving mothers seldom discuss how bad it hurts when people say the wrong things like, "You can always have another one." We rarely discuss how different husbands and wives grieve and how that can cause friction in a marriage. Mothers never discuss these things with the people who need to hear them. So this is why I'm writing about it.

Even I, as a mother, had no clue how difficult losing a child was until it happened to me. Do you know what else I learned? That I had not been supportive enough of other women I knew whose children passed away. If I'd only known how deep the pain was and the emotional toll it takes on a family. If only I'd known how agonizing it was to return the maternity clothes I'd already purchased and hear the sales clerk ask the reason for my return. If only I had an idea of how challenging it was to smile when people who had not heard the news would say, "So when are you due?" Oh, if only I had a clue. I would have held those ladies tight and cried with them, prayed with them, and given them my full support.

If you know someone who experiences the loss of a child, please ask how you can best support them. The worst thing you can do is turn your backs on them during the most vulnerable and painful times of their lives. The best comments were the most simple ones. "I love you." "I'm praying for you." "How can I help during this time?" While each woman may handle the death of a child differently, one thing is sure, they all need love and support. Even as the days pass, continue to offer encouragement. Birthdays and holidays are tough. The following Mothers Day I felt so guilty because there I was, blessed with three precious children, secretly dealing with feelings of depression because I was missing a child I once carried.

I am not one to always express my innermost feelings. I rarely discuss my pain. So why have I written so much and so in-depth about such a personal experience? Because I wish someone would have warned me. I wish I'd known ahead of time so I could have been more supportive of other moms.

They say time heals a broken heart; some grieving mothers may not agree. I believe you just eventually learn to handle the pain. The next year I experienced another miscarriage. I remember taking a week's vacation that summer so I did not have to hide my emotions while at work. I was bitter with God, and I was angry with myself. I felt as if my body failed me, my babies, and my husband. But as most mothers do, I worked through that bitterness and realized that there are some things in life I cannot control.

Thankfully, in 2015, I gave birth to my rainbow baby. Babies born after a miscarriage, stillbirth, or infant death are called rainbow babies, just as a rainbow appears in the sky following a storm. This life experience is why I'm an older mom with a toddler and a child soon entering her senior year of high school. I consider it an honor to share these experiences with others. I never thought I would be able to type these words, but I am thankful that God opened my eyes to the pain of miscarriage. I have been able to speak with so many women who have experienced early loss. If it were not for my pain, I would never be able to relate or minister to grieving mothers with genuine understanding.

If you have ever experienced the death of a child, allow me to say, I'm so sorry for your loss. Never let anyone make you feel guilty for grieving or for keeping the memory of your child alive. Take the time you need to heal but never forget that your life is still worth living. The pain from child loss is undeniably difficult. Losing a baby changes you forever. To carry a child on the inside of you is a real miracle. An even greater miracle is having the strength to endure when you are left with only a memory. You are a miracle.

It's Ok To Say No

Moms tend to be the busiest people on the planet. We are constantly on the go caring for our families and serving those around us. But even with our hectic schedules, many mothers have a difficult time saying no to requests that we know will max out our schedules. Whether it's a request from a friend, family member, the PTO, or a volunteer opportunity, we have a difficult time saying no, even when we are already stretched to capacity.

I have often heard that the busiest people may also be the least productive. It took me a while to grasp that concept, but I'm so grateful I now understand. In the past, I have become so busy that my effectiveness was completely diminished and I lost sight of my own purpose in life. As mothers, it is so easy to get caught up in fielding the requests and demands of others that we forget who we are and why we exist. Our personal goals and family objectives become an afterthought. We must remember that, sometimes, it's ok to say no. Although it's vital that we help others, we should never become so busy that we overlook our true purpose and calling.

My husband, Roc, is a devoted husband and father. He is also one of the most loving, generous, free-hearted men I have ever met. Because of his genuine love for people it has always been difficult for him to turn down requests from others no matter how big or small. For almost a decade I watched my husband give his all every single day, seven days a week, while being heavily involved in ministry. Each night he would drag himself home, drained, exhausted, and burnt-out from the busyness of the day. Roc's heart was in the right place because he desired to help others - but at what expense? Before long,

Roc was on the verge of complete burnout because he failed to invest in his own mental, physical, and emotional health.

One day he came to the realization that in order to save himself, he had to step back. He realized that there are times when saying no is necessary and in this case a matter of life and death.

Sometimes it's difficult to say no, especially when you truly want to save the world, but you must first protect yourself. If you are always willing to give, even at the expense of your own sanity and health, people will easily take advantage of your generosity. Your time is precious so it is vital to get rid of unnecessary obligations, prioritize your time, embrace balance, and learn to say no.

A Home is Meant to Be Lived In

Do you ever have family and friends who drop by unannounced? I grew up in a family where that was completely unacceptable. Living in Ohio, you always called before a visit just out of genuine respect. Since moving to SC, I'm convinced there is a different rule of southern hospitality.

Every time the sound of the doorbell echoed throughout my home, I would find myself scrambling to pick up toys, bottles and then scurry into the kitchen to hide the dirty dishes. You know that little warming drawer at the bottom of the stove? Well, yeah that was the perfect hiding spot. I mean, it was so much easier to keep a clean home before having children, but times drastically changed. Upon opening the door, my greeting would always end with the words, "please excuse the mess." I felt guilty that my home was not always spic and span. I mean it was never horrid, but there was just no way to keep it spotless with toddlers, no matter how hard I tried. From little fingerprints on the windows to a bucket full of dumped out Legos in the middle of the living room, I somehow felt a sense of embarrassment. But eventually, I stopped apologizing. I realized that visitors were in our space and in our home.

The more children I began to have, the more I understood that a home is meant to be lived in. Now, if you are a mom who is able to balance it all and keep your house above board, I applaud you! You are an example to the masses! I have certainly not reached that level and doubt I ever will. Our home is a place where children sometimes play ball, ride their scooters, and make instruments out of pots and pans. In our home, you will sometimes dodge a running toddler, step over a tricycle or walk carefully to avoid the broken crayons on the floor. Although I would love a self-cleaning house, I'm proud to have a home where children can just be children. As I type this, my tub is filled with Paw Patrol toys, dinosaurs, and mini fire trucks. But why should I feel guilty or ashamed when it's our home? It's our safe place and the only home in the world where we can be ourselves, without judgment.

The truth of the matter is, apologizing most likely draws more attention to the disarray that more than likely resembles your visitor's home. Now just in case you're wondering, I am training my children to be organized and tidy, but it's quite challenging in a home with six people. They are also trained in how to respect the homes of others who may prefer a much quieter and tidier atmosphere. Bottom line is, your home is your sanctuary, your place of refuge. Never apologize for creating an atmosphere in your home that's conducive to making lasting memories.

Confidence is Key

My fourth grader is truly one of a kind. She is confident, humorous, and lives life without any worries whatsoever. Alonna is self-assured and couldn't care less what anyone else thinks about her. When she picks out her own clothes, absolutely nothing matches! If I allowed her, Alonna would wear a Christmas shirt in the summer and an Easter dress at Christmas. Why? Because she's not concerned one bit about what her classmates think and is not in competition with anyone. She is who she is, and she makes no apologies for it.

One day I overheard Alonna arguing with her older sister. I couldn't quite make out what they were fussing about at the time, but all of a sudden Alonna belts out...I'm a genius with a capital J. The sound of laughter filled our home. She had no clue why that was so funny, and to be honest, she didn't care. She laughed just as hard as everyone else in the room, because even in her inability to spell genius correctly, she was still confident that she was a genius. You see, when it comes to living life, Alonna does not focus on negative reactions from others. She's able to cancel out the noise from the cynics and live her best life. There is so much that mothers could take away from this. As moms, we often lose confidence because of the way motherhood changes us physically, mentally, and even emotionally. Our insecurities cause us to compare ourselves with other women and lose the confidence we once had. Just remember that even with your flaws and imperfections, you have a unique journey and a specific purpose in your child's life that no one else can fill. You may not parent like others around you, and your values may be different from those of your friends and family. That makes you no less of a mom. Choose to be confident in who you are and your role as a mother. Confidence is a beautiful thing! You are only in competition with yourself – aiming to be better today than you were yesterday. Just like Alonna, aim to be a genius with a capital J.

Take Time to Capture Precious Memories

Taking a trip to our local movie theatre is one of my family's favorite pastimes. We all know the ticket costs are astronomical and the concession prices are absolutely absurd. I hate to admit it, but I am famous for sneaking in candy and snacks into the movies because, let's face it, who wants to pay $20 for a large popcorn and a drink. One summer day I decided to take my son Elijah to the movies. He was around the age of three or four at the time. Well, this particular day Elijah decided he wanted me to bring him a sandwich and a juice box in the movies. Of course, I obliged and filled my purse to capacity. Upon arrival at the theatre, Elijah stood patiently in line. We handed the employee our tickets and waited for him to return our stubs. All of a sudden Elijah gasped! He looked up at me with those big brown eyes and yelled, "Oh no, mommy you forgot our sandwiches!" I elbowed him to try to get him to hush but it was too late. We all just laughed.

These are moments I never want to forget. The memories motherhood brings truly warms my heart. There are times I wish time would stand still. Instead, the days pass swiftly, and the memories quickly fade. I've never been the scrap booking type of mom, but maybe I should have been. With four children, sometimes, the details of their lives all run together. My kids will ask....who started walking first? Which one of us was potty trained first? Ummmmmmm? Sometimes I just have to say whatever comes to my mind! Awful, I know. So now, I've started journaling stories and memories I want to hold close. It's great to keep those memories fresh and also a great instrument for generations to come. I would love to know some of the thoughts, ideas, and day-to-day life activities of my great-grandparents and even generations past.

We are very fortunate to have cell phones now to capture so many unforgettable moments. A recent video of my child's daycare adventures tops the list. My husband used to always poke fun at my son Josiah, because as soon as he walks in the door at home, he strips his clothes off to make himself comfortable. My husband would say, "Are you naked? You can't just walk around naked!" Josiah thought that was the funniest thing. He would just laugh and run straight to the couch to relax. From the moment he learned to dress and undress himself, we had to make him keep some form of clothes on. Well, the first day I took Josiah to preschool he stood in the hallway crying and screaming..."I just want to go home and get naked! I just want to be naked!" It was sad, funny, and also embarrassing because I'm sure the teachers and parents wondered exactly what would prompt a two-year-old to say something like that. I'm surprised someone did not contact DSS. But those are memories I never want to forget.

Moms, we can't rely on our overworked minds to remember those special moments. Find the time to jot down the priceless remarks your children make. When they're older, you will all enjoy looking back on their journey and the moments that brought you so much joy.

Children May Not Fully Comprehend Your Sacrifices

As a young child, weekday mornings were very hectic for my family, to say the least. Our morning routines were pretty typical of a family preparing to arrive at school in a timely fashion. We would drag ourselves out of bed, shower, dress, and enjoy a quick breakfast before heading out the door.

At one point in our lives, we attended a private school that unfortunately did not provide transportation for students. So my father took it upon himself to drive us to school every morning. He also helped provide transportation for other children in the city who otherwise would not have been able to attend this particular school. There was no carpool agreement. We never took turns riding with other parents. As is typical of my father, he just took it upon himself to make that sacrifice to help other families. As a middle school child, I had no understanding of what he sacrificed to fit that into his busy schedule. I never recognized how tiring it must have been for him to work late into the evenings and still transport a car full of children to school before 7:30.

My sister and I would joke about his gruesome black coffee breath in the mornings. We laughed about running out of gas sometimes and flaunted an attitude when he was late picking us up in the afternoons. I never really considered that he was juggling work, family, and finances until I began to do the same. Like many parents, there were times that my father worked a full-time position and also juggled several part-time jobs just to make ends meet. We never went without.

As I prepare home-cooked meals for my own children, I am reminded of my mother's sacrifice to always prepare made-from-scratch meals for my family. We were so blessed, but as I child, I did not fully recognize that. I never fully understood these sacrifices until I began conquering the carpool line, basketball practice, soccer practice, and chorus concerts all in one day – all while trying to maintain a career. I know that children appreciate what we do, but I also understand there is no way for them to fully comprehend the depth of our sacrifices at this point in their lives. As a child, you just expect to be taken care of. You assume there will be food on the table, clothes to wear, and to always get from point A to point B. But as your children begin to enter the world of adulthood, your sacrifices will become much clearer. As they mature, they will think back on the days that you ran from sun-up to sundown giving your all.

I do take time to explain to my children that often the sacrifices we make are not always necessary. We go above and beyond because of our love for them. My oldest child is 16 now and is already becoming much more aware of the sacrifices we make. I believe her appreciation and that of my other children will only grow stronger. My sincere prayer is that my children will never forget the love and dedication they constantly receive and that they will pass that same devotion on to their children and for generations to come.

Just Go With the Flow

Not only am I a proud mother, I am the proud aunt to two beautiful children, Mariah and Maxwell. Well, just before Maxwell was born, I made plans to travel from South Carolina to Ohio to witness his beautiful birth. We'd planned to drive so that the entire family could be there for this joyous occasion. Only, Maxwell decided to arrive early. Just moments after receiving that unexpected phone call, we quickly threw random clothes in a bag and tossed our extremely disorganized suitcases in the back of my husband's truck. I had no idea what my children had packed, and this time I really didn't care. Road trip! We made a quick fast-food run to grab the family a meal and then hit the road. Everyone was so excited and could barely wait to arrive in Cleveland. But about 30 minutes into the trip, on I-85, my husband hit two of the biggest potholes we had ever seen. We gasped. The tires began to deflate, and so did our plans.

While this story is not a normal everyday occurrence, you know as a mom, even some of our most well thought out plans are often rerouted. We have our little organizers and planners and put so much thought into each day. But things rarely seem to happen as we design. With children, you never know when your plans will be turned upside down. So you just take a deep breath, smile, and make the adjustment, just as we did that evening. I learned that when I become frustrated because plans change; I stress out, my attitude rubs off on my family, and in the end, the situation still hasn't changed. In fact, it only gets worse.

I can remember so many times when I was right on schedule, had my children fed, dressed, and secure in their car seats, one of them would always have to use the bathroom. Are you serious?! I'd be forced to go back inside, and guess what? Now we're late. I would start fussing, my children would begin to cry, and I still wouldn't be on time.

So, the older I've gotten, I've learned to remain calm and just make the necessary adjustments for my own sanity. Becoming frustrated and angry only produces a negative atmosphere that adversely affects you and those around you, including your children.

Negative energy only makes a difficult situation even harder. That night, as we pulled over at the nearest exit, we chose to remain positive. We sat in the car and laughed until the tow truck arrived. When he dropped us off at our home, we grabbed our luggage out of the truck and just stood there in disbelief as our vehicle was towed away.

I could have easily cried and expressed the disappointment I felt on the inside, but I knew this was also a teachable moment for my children. When life begins to take a different turn, put on your signal light and keep trucking.

One week later, we eventually made it to Ohio and met my nephew. This experience, like so many others in my life, reminded me that I am not always in control.

I want my life to be a certain way and I work very hard to achieve that. But, there are times when I must surrender to situations that I have no control over, trust God, and keep moving forward. My goal is to focus, readjust, maintain a positive attitude, and show my children unexpected changes are just a part of life. Life's interferences may be difficult, but sometimes we just have to grin and bear it.

Live Your Life Backwards

There is nothing more heartbreaking than when a loved one passes away. Our lives are changed forever, and we are suddenly left with only memories of the one we held so dear. Death is a subject most of us would rather avoid although we know it is inevitable. When we no longer walk this earth our family and friends will recall how you made them feel and how much you impacted their lives.

I often wonder how my family and friends will remember me when my mission on this earth is complete. If I pass away first, will my children recall moments that brought them joy? Will they recall a nagging mom or a mother with a gentle and empathetic heart? Will they remember a mother whose priorities were work, hanging with friends, or a momma who always found time for her children? How do you think your obituary will read? How do you want your family and future generations to remember you? Jot it down and live backwards.

Do you want your children and family to remember you as a dedicated mother? Then be one. Do you want them to remember you as a giving person? Then give. Do you want them to remember you as a loving person? Then love. Do you want to be remembered as someone who changed the world? Then change it. It's that simple. Write your own memorial and make it your blueprint, your guide, your goal in life. Don't let anything hinder you from being the amazing mother God designed you to be.

Your children, no matter how old they are, deserve to have significant memories of their time with you. There are many females who did not grow up in a loving home. They either carry that negativity into their own households or choose to break the mold. No matter your path, we are all called to greatness, but we allow life's circumstances and the demons of our past to impede our purpose. Rise about it all. How you live your life today will impact your children, your grandchildren, and generations to come. How will you be remembered?

Compassion Is Best Taught By Example

We live in such a self-centered, egocentric society. It is becoming increasingly difficult to raise my children in a way that causes them to empathize with their peers and cultivate generosity toward others. From the time children enter this world, they consider their own desires to be a priority. Even before they are able to speak, babies communicate their wants by crying, pouting, whining, and throwing tantrums. While that is pretty typical for the average young child, we should, at some point, grow out of this stage. Eventually, the "all about me" attitude should be replaced with care and compassion for those around us. Some children are able to demonstrate empathy naturally but others have to be taught.

The overwhelming theme in this society is, it's all about me. Twenty years ago it would be unheard of to take a "self"ie, but that's the world we live in. When we post selfies, we gain satisfaction when our friends 'like' our photos and comment on how amazing we look. I have nothing at all against selfies, but at some point, our focus must be refocused. In our daily lives, there are times when the attention should be on others who are hurting and in need of the necessities to live comfortably and make ends meet.

The best way to raise children with a heart for compassion and love for others is to demonstrate those very characteristics. It is a priority of ours to sow our time, talent, and treasures into the needs of our community and make sure our children do the same. During the summers we help deliver meals to the homebound through a wonderful organization, Mobile Meals. My children literally fuss and fight over who gets to ring the doorbell first and who gets to hand over the meals. But if they're going to fight for something, I'd rather them compete for an opportunity to serve others.

Children need to see that while they are eager to receive the newest name-brand shoes, there are others without any shoes at all. This generation needs to understand that the real world does not revolve around them and that teaching needs to begin at an early age. It starts with simple lessons and books about sharing and giving to others. Children also observe how you respond and give to others in need. Likewise, they listen to the comments you make about others who have less than you do, so also watch your words. If you look down on other people, your children will grow up to do the same thing. Teaching empathy to our children will help reduce bullying and discrimination. No matter what we are blessed to possess, we are no better than the next. I want my children to look for ways to bless others and to have a heart for their community and those around them. It's never our job to judge others because we never know what the person next to us has endured.

Compassion is best taught by example. Chances are, egotistical and self-absorbed parents will raise young people who grow up to be the same way. Let's show our children how not to live a "selfie" life but point the camera in the right direction and focus on those around them.

Parent Now
Friend Later

When my first child, Mikayla, was born, I was not only birthing a new member into our young family, I felt like I would soon have a new friend. What mom does not look forward to sharing secrets, salon dates, and shopping trips with their beautiful daughter? As Mikayla began to grow older, make mistakes, and experience childhood dilemmas, I knew that being a friend was not necessarily the best choice. She had plenty of childhood friends. What Mikayla needed was a mother.

Many moms aspire to be best friends with their children, but in my experience, it is more significant to first be a parent. We are the authority figures in their lives here to lead, guide, and raise them to become loving, responsible adults. This means that the relationship with your child will most likely include unpopular and difficult decisions such as discipline, consequences for behaviors, and setting guidelines they may not understand. That's all a part of motherhood.

Don't misunderstand, my children and I have wonderful relationships. We spend quality time together and they are fully confident that they can talk to me about anything. At least I think they do! We certainly have our unpleasant moments, but if you catch us on a good day, it would appear that we were the best of friends. But there are times, I have to draw the line and remind them who is in charge. For example, I keep a close eye on their online activity and monitor screen time for my youngest ones. While some may consider this an invasion of privacy, I believe it's my right and my responsibility as a parent to help protect my children.

When I was younger, I never considered my mother to be a friend. We had a wonderful relationship, and she took amazing care of my sisters and me. But no matter how close we became I knew my boundaries. I knew there were some things I could say to my friends, that I would never be allowed to say to my mother. After I graduated from high school, our relationship began to change. Somewhere along the way she has become the best female friend I've ever been blessed with.

Considering your child to be your friend has been the subject of debate for some time now. As the mother of your household, you must choose what's best for you and your family. If you are able to balance being a friend and an effective mother to your child, then by all means, go for it! In my experiences, children have a difficult time having a disciplinarian as a close friend.

Mikayla is now 16 years old, and I feel our relationship beginning to shift. I recently took her for a well check-up visit. While waiting to visit the doctor, we were filling out the mounds of dreaded paperwork. Beside the parent signature, there was a line with the words, relationship to patient. Mikayla said, just put friend. She didn't know, but I actually began to tear up. My heart was touched because I know our relationship is transitioning, just as mine did with my mother.

Regardless of how you choose to raise your children, there is no doubt that friendship is a beautiful reward of motherhood. We are immensely blessed to have the opportunity to build loving relationships with our babies. As we carefully guide them toward an independent lifestyle, take great care to create unbreakable bonds that will stand the test of time.

Get a Grip on Fickle Finances

Like many women, shopping is without a doubt, one of my most favorite pastimes. I am, by no stretch of the imagination, a fashionista. I just consider shopping to be somewhat therapeutic, especially if I can manage to get away without the kids. Whether it's sorting through a sales rack inside a brick and mortar or shopping online, I do not discriminate.

I'm not too sure if shopping can be a part of a person's genetic make-up but I am quite certain that I inherited this gene from my mother. I remember once, my mom and I decided to visit a salon for a quick manicure. We'd told the men, who were assigned babysitting duties, we would return in two hours. Well, we decided to take a quick walk through Dillard's first and became distracted by the red tags. We had so much fun trying on clothes that we lost track of time. My mom and I literally spent the entire two hours in that store and never made it to the salon. We returned with our hands full of Dillard's deals and horrible looking nails.

Shopping is like my love language to my family. I love to walk in the house with new clothes and shoes and see the smiles on my children's faces. Now in my defense, I've never been a huge spender. I rarely purchase anything at regular price but, I have a habit of purchasing items we do not need just because they're on sale. But now, as my children are getting older, I'm beginning to change my spending habits and focus on the bigger picture. I know that in a few years my children will need finances for college, living expenses, weddings and from what I've been told, the list never ends even after they move out.

When my husband and I are off the scene, I want to leave my children with a level of financial backing. For this reason, we have now established a strict family budget, a college savings plan, and purchased life insurance for every member of the household. That may seem minor for some well-established households but we are making progress one step at a time. We are on the road to paying off any and all debt. A few years ago my sister introduced us to the philosophy of businessman and author Dave Ramsey. We have adopted some of those principles into our lifestyle by counting every single dollar, getting out of debt, and preparing for the future. I am still working on breaking some of those spending habits!

Neither my husband nor I grew up with a silver spoon in our mouths. We have worked hard to provide a stable life for our children but both lacked the training others had about financial management and decision-making. I pray that my husband and I are blessed to live a long and prosperous life, but whenever we transition, I want to leave my children with more than memories. I do not want them to struggle financially or live from paycheck to paycheck, so I'm trying to teach them positive spending and saving habits. I'm not too sure how well it's working though.

My oldest has a part-time job and her little check is gone almost before she gets it. I just want them to understand that the spending decisions and investments we make today will affect their lives in the future. Regardless of your income, I encourage you to keep track of your spending habits, saving habits and also make wise investments. Most financial advisors will hold an initial meeting with you at no cost. Make small steps toward leaving a monetary legacy that will help your children build a strong future of their own.

Be Particular About Who Watches Your Children

Have you watched the news lately? Horrifying, right? As a former broadcast journalist, I have always had a love for current events but the recent headlines are horrifying. We used to turn on the news in the mornings while getting prepared for work and school, but with the frightening and bazaar stories we hear today, it's almost depressing to watch. The news is filled with stories about children being sold into the slave market, school and church shootings on the rise, and crime of preposterous proportions.

What's wrong with the world we live in? It's quite daunting to raise children in a world that is becoming increasingly violent as the days pass. We must be on high alert when it comes to our children. I'm not proposing that you live in fear, but I am suggesting that you keep a very close eye on your children and the places they visit. You are their first line of defense.

Children are incredibly trusting and naive. We must ask the tough questions they don't want to answer and check out the close friends they hang-out with. My children hate that I interrogate them about their choices of friends, but one day they will understand. No one else in the world loves your child as much as you do. No one else is going to protect them like you do. Never leave that job to someone else.

There also seems to be a rise in reports of sexual assault and abuse cases. We are too trusting with family members and close friends. Statistics show that the majority of sexual abuse cases involve family members we trust. Mommas, it is your duty to ask the tough questions. We must speak with our children about inappropriate touching. We must speak with our children about not being in situations where they could be accused of or be a victim of sexual assault. Being up-front with your children minimizes their chances of becoming victims. If we do not protect our own children, who will? This is a subject that I am extremely passionate about. There are far too many cases of abuse happening because parents are not diligent enough and are far too trusting of others with their children. Abuse is occurring in churches, daycares, and many unexpected places, so educate your children from a young age and ask lots of questions.

While I do believe in the power of praying over our children, as parents, we also have a responsibility to do everything in our power to protect them. Get to know the other adults and young people in your children's lives. Once abuse occurs, it is too late to turn back the hands of time. The damage will have already been done. This is a crazy world we live in. If you don't believe me, just turn on the news. Mommas do whatever it takes to protect and keep your children safe. Do not leave them in the wrong hands and never allow anyone to make you feel guilty about your decisions. When it comes to protecting your children, be a warrior without compromise.

Place an Emphasis on Integrity & Family Values

In today's society, honesty and integrity appear to be a thing of the past. Dignitaries fall and companies fail because even the most accomplished and gifted leaders forsake the truth. As mothers, we can no longer rely on the world to impart and illustrate true character. If we fail to set the example for our sons and daughters, the world will become their moral compass. Your family values should be discussed and demonstrated.

How can you teach your children the importance of honesty, loyalty, and morality, when it is rarely demonstrated even among our world leaders? For this reason, we must be committed to teach and practice respectable characteristics. Just as mothers should strive to set an example for their children, our sons and daughters will likewise become an example amongst their peers.

In 2005 my husband and I planned a family vacation to visit a popular amusement park. Finances were pretty tight, but we were enthusiastic about experiencing something new as a young family. Upon arrival at the gate, I stood there shocked that only children two and under were free. My daughter Mikayla had recently celebrated her third birthday, which meant an additional $100 I was not prepared to pay. As we reached the entrance, an employee asked my daughter's age. I softly replied, "two." In my heart I was immediately convicted.

I was hoping my daughter would not overhear our conversation. I knew she'd belt out, "I'm three." You see, we'd been practicing that together. The employee asked again, "You sure she's two?" I replied a little louder this time but with a slight attitude, "Yes, she's two." My daughter looked up at me but never said a word. As we walked through the park entrance, I felt ashamed and embarrassed. Even though my daughter was so young, I prayed that this moment would be completely erased from her memory. To me, this was much bigger than just a lie. As her mother, I was giving her permission to be dishonest. I was showing her that it was acceptable to be deceitful if she was ever in a difficult situation.

Integrity is rarely learned from a textbook. It's taught in the home. It's up to us to instill positive traits in our sons and daughters, even at a young age. Making the right choice is not always easy, but choosing to be unethical can have devastating repercussions. We see it nearly every day. Politicians, preachers, teachers, athletes, and other leaders make erroneous choices and intentionally lie to camouflage their past mistakes. Often, they lose everything they worked so hard to build.

No child is perfect, but when my children are honest about making mistakes, I tend to be much more lenient. They are still disciplined, but knowing they chose to speak up, gives me a glimpse of hope that there is still some good in them. As a mother, you can help restore character in this generation of young people. I believe we can change the world one child at a time.

Children Are Human Too

I casually asked my twelve-year-old son what advice I should offer other moms. Without hesitation, he responded, "Don't punish your children the first time they make mistakes." I initially thought, "Well that's pretty sensible advice, son." Later my mind revisited that conversation. Was I the cause of his swift recommendation?

Like most parents, my husband and I set pretty high standards for our children. We make clear our expectations and expect them to follow suit. In our quest to raise them right, we forget, they too, are human beings incapable of perfection. But how we react when our children make mistakes is a major component of their development. If we set unreasonable expectations, they will most likely retreat. On several occasions, I have heard my son make comments such as, "I never do anything right." No mother wants her child to feel that way. In our house, there are no excuses for messing up. You admit you failed and make it right. I admit, at times I can be quite demanding. But there are times God quickly reminds me of the numerous times I, too, needed mercy. He causes me to recall specific times when I have been in their position. Children are humans with feelings and emotions, who need understanding and empathy. There are certainly times when young people need tough love, but other times, loving guidance is a much better remedy.

The famous poet, Maya Angelou, once said, "I've learned that people will forget what you said, people will forget what you did, but people will never forget how you made them feel." Sometimes we speak to our children as if they have no feelings at all. One day, they will grow up to become adults who will remember exactly how you made them feel. Do not allow the stresses of your life to affect the way you treat and respond to them. When you become frustrated with your children, take a deep breath and try using a bit of patience, because no one is perfect. As Elijah believes, sometimes we all need a little grace.

Learn from Your Children

Motherhood is one of the greatest ministries to ever exist. We completely dedicate our lives to raising the children God entrusts us with, in hopes that they will one day grow up to positively change the world. Mothers have such an awesome, yet frightening, responsibility to teach and reach our children in ways that no one else can. I consistently push them and motivate them toward greatness because that's how they will reach their full potential. What's so strange is that in my steadfast journey to inspire them, I too am inspired.

Their faith in humanity encourages me to find the good in the world. Their love of life reminds me to relax and enjoy the journey. Their diverse friendships remind me that there is hope for the human race. Their notice of ordinary pleasures reminds me to appreciate the simple things in life. Their innocent laughter reminds me that happiness is a choice. I know my mission is to impact them, but I am such a better person because they entered my life. So many times I feel like I've failed them, but they forgive without even being asked. One second they are quarreling and the next moment they are best friends. They inspire me to love deeply and forgive quickly.

When I was a young child, I never worried about my safety. In the 70's it was almost unheard of for a gunman to enter a church or school. It never even crossed my mind. They inspire me to be brave. When my toddler grabs my finger or offers hugs and kisses without being asked, I am reminded that I am loved. The timeliness of his spontaneous compassion seems as if God himself arranged it.

My children inspire me to become a better person and give life everything I have. I know they are watching me. I know they depend on me. I know they are counting on my love. So if you ever feel like giving up, take a moment to observe the innocence of your children, listen to the purity in their laughter, and take notice of how quickly they recover from life's challenges. You, too, will be inspired and encouraged to persevere. Inspiration is not a one-way street.

Discipline Should Come From A Place of Love

Discipline is such a controversial topic that I dare not attempt to educate you on the specifics of reprimanding your own children. The never-ending debate over the acceptable use of corporal punishment is such an emotional one. Both parents and doctors have strong feelings either in favor of or against using spankings, time-outs, and withholding privileges as a way of disciplining children. Regardless of the methods you choose, it's vital to remember that chastisement should always come from a place of love.

Children certainly have a way of testing their parents and pushing the limits and boundaries we have set in place. Whether you are dealing with temper tantrums, unruly behavior, or ungratefulness, discipline is a necessary and effective tool. But when you respond and discipline out of a heart of anger, your attempts to correct behavior may be unsuccessful and full of regrets for both you and your child. I'm sure we have all experienced this.

Over the years, I have learned to take a moment for myself before I react. It's amazing how a deep breath and 15 minutes to cool down helps me properly process the situation. I try to understand the reasoning behind my child's decisions and decide on consequences that will be the most impactful. After all, the real purpose of discipline is to help our children understand that there are consequences for inappropriate behavior. Again, I am not advocating one particular type of correction, but I am encouraging you to discipline with a heart full of love.

Love does not end when your child makes choices that you disagree with. Love does not end when your child misbehaves. That's when love is most important.

We are not called to be bullies. We are called to love, nurture, support, and impart truth and wisdom. Be sure that you have clearly communicated your expectations and if they are not met, clearly communicate why discipline is necessary. Children need consistency in a structured and loving environment. When your child recognizes the depth of your love, even discipline can be an affectionate experience for everyone involved. They may not enjoy the consequences of their actions, but they will appreciate the heart behind it.

Take Time to Invest in Your Marriage

It's Friday night, and I lay in bed silently. In the still of the dark night, the thoughts in my mind are explosive. My toddler has, once again, made his way into our bed; perfectly tucked between my husband and me. My spouse, exhausted from the day, has drifted into another world. On this evening, my mind is filled with the business of the weekend's schedule. Basketball, soccer, church, work; the list appears to be infinite. If only my mind would accept the rest it so desperately deserves. My thoughts are too consumed with the busyness of tomorrow to relax from the demands of today. There never seems to be enough time to accomplish it all.

Whether you are married, divorced, single, or widowed, everyone's family structure is different and comes with its own set of challenges. In our home, most days are spent with our energies entirely focused on caring for our children, managing our careers, ministry, and everything else in between. A hectic schedule rarely leaves much time for my husband and me to spend quality time with one another. Dates nights are rare, and daily conversations are often consumed with family and work matters.

One of the biggest challenges of our marriage is creating balance and finding time to intentionally invest in strengthening our relationship. We are not fortunate enough to have nearby family and friends whose schedules are not already consumed, so we juggle it all. It's a familiar story for many families that can be both physically and mentally exhausting. We chose marriage, and we chose to have children. Therefore we must choose to invest in both.

The love my husband and I have for each other is unyielding. Neither of us questions our commitment, but we are both guilty of forsaking each other for the sake of our children. I am most likely the guiltier partner. If only the Lord had given us 34-hour days! Finding time alone, without the children, will always seem impossible, but we must make that a high priority. We have literally paid a babysitter and left the house with absolutely no plans in place. Sometimes we will run out for ice cream and just sit in the car talking for hours. It's an opportunity for us to bond and share what's on our hearts. Somehow much of our conversation still focuses on the children. One day my husband and I will get better at this dating thing though.

If you are married, part of being a great parent is taking the time to invest in your relationship with your husband. Your children need to see what a healthy marriage is supposed to look like. We are the foundation upon which our children grow and flourish. Make sure that foundation is strong and unbreakable.

Relax & Enjoy the Journey

There is not much more rewarding than hearing the laughter of a child. Regardless of what my day brings, the stress I encounter, or the existing circumstances in my life, hearing my children laugh reminds me that I am incredibly blessed. Innocent sounds of jovialness cause me to consider that maybe, just maybe, life is not as harsh as it sometimes appears. Stress has the devastating ability to drain your joy and happiness, but only if you choose that particular path. We can choose to be overwhelmed by life's encounters or, like children, laugh in the face of adversity and simply enjoy the journey.

For so many of us, it's so easy to become consumed with everyday errands, crowded calendars, and tantalizing to-do lists. We work from sun-up until sun-down and still rarely accomplish the laundry list of items we intend to complete. In the midst of our daily tasks and responsibilities, we seldom take time to relax and relish in the joys of motherhood. We focus so much of our energy trying to survive that we lose our ability to actually thrive.

I've learned that no matter how well you plan or execute your daily obligations, the work will always be there. So I challenge you to put down the list and take a few moments to laugh with your child, enjoy a heart-to-heart exchange, or create something together. Observe their seamless smiles and allow the splendid sounds of their laughter to resonate within you.

Although you may feel overwhelmed by obligations and overcome by obstacles, take a moment to acknowledge and appreciate the blessings in your life. Young children laugh and play as if they have not one care in the world. If only we could learn that lesson. When we choose to become overwhelmed and bogged down, we are unable to enjoy the life we have with our children. We will miss the simple things in life that remind us of God's love for us and the love we have for our families. Life is short. Focus on the people and things that truly matter and deserve your energy.

Spend Time with Your Children Individually

Being a mother of four is the best job I 'never' dreamed of. That's right. I've always had a special love for children, but never did I imagine myself being a mother of four. But here I am, in love with a house full of little humans I've been entrusted with. Considering all our ups and downs, I have but one regret; as a mother, my time is stretched so thin it is rare that I am able to spend quality time with my children individually. This is such an important part of knowing who our children really are and understanding their individual needs.

My husband and I have intentionally chosen to place a priority on family time. More than anything, we want our children to know that they are valued and loved and a part of something special. But we also desire that each one feel treasured as an individual, not just as a member of our household. Every child is unique, but it's difficult to grasp their distinct strengths and weaknesses when they are only displayed in a group or family setting.

The greatest gift from our one-on-one time is the ability to connect through meaningful conversations. Giving children undivided attention allows them to express their fears and concerns without the pressure of judgment from their siblings. I had no idea that my twelve-year-old son was already stressing about his future and what major he would choose in college. I mean, seriously worried that making a B in math would literally crush his career plans. He'd made random comments about it amongst family, but his sisters always thought it was hilarious. But when we spent time alone, I discovered this was a genuine concern for him that needed to be addressed.

Recently, one afternoon I noticed that my happy-go-lucky nine-year-old was growing pretty cranky. She was snapping at her baby brother every chance she had. We told her to spend some time alone to think about her behavior. After about an hour, I decided she and I would just take a ride. Before we made it out of our neighborhood, she was in tears. She poured out her little heart, and I knew then, the negative attitude she displayed was much deeper than the surface. I learned that her attitude, was simply attention-seeking behavior. She needed to be heard, she wanted to be understood, and she too desired to feel important. But her three-year-old brother was stealing the show.

I've read stories where parents travel with their children each year to some exotic places. But I've discovered that trips to the grocery store work just as well. Expeditions to Publix and Kohl's are where my teenager keeps me up-to-date on all of her high-school drama.

Even as women, we want to be loved and desire to feel treasured for who we are as individuals. Our children are no different. Carving time out of your busy schedule for a game of basketball helps boost your child's self-confidence. A trip to the movie theatre says you are important enough to put the work aside. You will be amazed how devoting time for each child creates an unbreakable bond and a world of discovery.

We All Have Bad Days

Can I be frank with you? There are so many times I feel like the greatest failure of a mother. Please, no judgment here. I'm sure you've been there before. I have literally tried to run away, but my attempts to hide in a dark and silent bathroom are inevitably interrupted. "Hey, mom, are you in there?" I sit quietly, wishing I had splurged for a more lavish toilet seat with that extra soft cushion. My time is running short. I peak underneath the bathroom door to see if the coast is clear, but my eyes are met by little feet waiting for me to return to reality. But I refuse. I'm waiting it out. I deserve time alone! I hear them walk away, but realize it's only to develop a Plan B. I hear whispers as they slide a little piece of paper beneath the bathroom door. The writing resembles a ransom note of sorts, but simply says, "May we please have a snac?" I open the door and yell as loudly as I can, "Can mommy PLEASE catch a break. I'm exhausted and can't even use the restroom without you bothering me!" "And by the way, that's NOT how you spell SNACK!" I slammed the door. As those words are leaving my mouth, the guilt in my heart quickly began to intensify. It's too late though. I can almost envision myself running to the stage, "And the award for the worst mother of the year goes to....Cynthia Robinson!" The crowd cheers.

It was just one of those days: I'm cranky, the children have been continuously at each other's throats, their rooms are disastrous, the laundry pile is growing by leaps and bounds, and I literally feel that if one more, just one more thing is added to my to-do list, I'm going to lose it. Am I the only mother who ever reaches a boiling point? Absolutely, not. The well-put together moms in magazines are rarely authentic and seldom share the areas in which they fall short. But the truth is, we all do. The effort, energy, and efficiency it takes to survive motherhood are, at times, overwhelming. But we rarely show it or have genuine dialogue about it. On the outside, looking in, we appear to have it all together. But deep down inside we feel so inadequate. We wonder if we are really making the impact we'd hope to make. On those days we exchange patience for crabby exchanges with our kids, we worry that they will be scarred for life.

Motherhood is indeed a beautiful thing, but there are days when, to be quite honest, motherhood is not quite as picturesque as it appears. I've thought so many times, "Are you even qualified to write this book?" "Do you really have the audacity to give other mothers advice?" But as I contemplate the realities of my own experiences, I am reminded that somewhere there is an overwhelmed, exhausted, cantankerous mother barely holding her head above water. Somewhere there is a guilt-ridden mother, with a heart of gold, who finds it impossible to make positive connections with her child. Somewhere there is a tearful mother managing motherhood without the support of a loving spouse she'd dreamed of raising her children with. Whatever your story, you all need to know that you are not alone.

Please do not interpret this chapter as an attempt to paint a negative picture of motherhood. I'm merely choosing to expose its realities and truths. Many see motherhood through rose-colored glasses, but there are times the shades must come off. Regardless of your age, experience level, or faith, being a mother is a tough job. Every stage of development comes with its own set of challenges: infants with sleeping inconsistencies, toddlers and tantrums, elementary-age adjustments, middle-school madness, high-school hang-ups, college-age confusion, and adulthood adjustments. Whatever the age or stage, mothers are there every step of the way. I've discovered that stress and high-intensity levels often come from a lack of self-care and overextending ourselves. Motherhood can be mentally, physically, and emotionally draining, but you will survive every phase. When you consider all that we manage to accomplish each day, mothers are strong, fierce, and relentless. We are powerful and manage more than most executives deal with each day. Having a bad day doesn't make you a bad mother. It makes you human.

Teach Your Children To Be Grateful

One of my biggest pet peeves is the lack of gratitude in today's society. Don't misunderstand, this is not a stab at the younger generation; it's a character flaw I've witnessed even among many adults. A well-mannered thank-you is almost as extinct as the dinosaurs my son explores on YouTube. Ever hold a door for someone, and they just cruise on in without saying one word? It's as if you owed them that courteous gesture! On the surface, that particular example may seem pretty minor, but it's a reflection of a much bigger epidemic; a self-centered and ungrateful world.

Over the years, I've witnessed the world's focus on gratitude decrease, while the emphasis on self and materialism has increased. We have become so accustomed to our routines and lifestyles, that we rarely express appreciation for the basics in life. If we are not expressing gratitude, how can we expect our children to learn that concept?

Ralph Waldo Emerson once said, "Cultivate the habit of being grateful for every good thing that comes to you and to give thanks continuously. And because all things have contributed to your advancement, you should include all things in your gratitude." Before my children could even speak, I encouraged them to display gratefulness. "Say thank you," I'd tell them. But it's difficult to teach children who have always had their basic needs met to be grateful for all things.

Recently, on our morning commute to school, one of my children blurted out, "This is already a horrible day. It's just horrible." Having to take two tests that day was the root of this statement. But that negative, ungrateful comment really lit a fire underneath my husband. He began to express to our children things they should be grateful for. In no particular order, my husband energetically listed their blessings back-to-back-to-back, barely taking a breath between each word: Life, health, strength, breath, sound mind, active limbs, running water, heat, carpet, a home, clothes, shoes, food, family, love; the list literally continued the entire five miles to school. As my husband called them out, I believe everyone in that car felt convicted. We all take so much for granted.

Sometimes it takes a global world perspective for our children to understand that not everyone wakes up to the basic necessities in life. My husband is involved in local and overseas missions work. He recalls children in other countries lining up for $1 flip-flops the mission's team was passing out, yet, some children are preconditioned to think it's a necessity to only have the latest brand shoes. There are children in the United States without clean running water, but for us, taking a shower is nothing special, just part of our daily routine.

I remember, years ago, visiting a church where my father-in-law spoke. Following the service, we were all invited for a reception in the fellowship hall. We were escorted to our seats where members kindly brought a variety of hors d'oeuvres to our table. One precious middle-age woman brought over a tray of petite chicken-salad sandwiches. I placed a couple on my children's plates and then my own. I kindly thanked her for her hospitality. My son Elijah, who was about three at the time, looked up and said, "Thank you for these chicken-salad sandwiches that we don't like!" I could have literally crawled underneath that table. I was afraid to look up to even see the expression on her face. We joke about it now, but that night, his expression of ungratefulness was beyond humiliating.

Although he was only three, this embarrassing moment reminded me of my obligation to impart gratefulness (and manners) into the hearts of my children. How can we teach them to appreciate life? Display gratefulness in your home by consistently vocalizing what you are thankful for. Remind your children that not everyone has the necessary provisions in life by allowing them to participate in local service learning projects.

Provide your child's necessities, but have them sacrifice and work to earn some of their wants. I've often heard the saying that your attitude will determine your altitude. There is much truth to this statement. Regardless of how difficult life is, there is always something to be thankful for. Having an attitude of gratitude will take you far in life. Regardless of where we live, the brand of clothes you wear, or the chicken-salad sandwiches you eat, always be grateful!

It's OK To Ask for Help

I unequivocally admit I am certainly not an expert in this area. Whether I'm juggling family-related business or managing my career, I would much rather do the job myself than petition help. It's so difficult to find people who are always reliable and genuinely willing to help, so I usually set out on a mission to conquer tasks on my own. I don't mind helping others, but I find it incredibly challenging to accept help, especially when I have to ask for it.

When I was pregnant with my second child, I remember so vividly waking up with my pajama bottoms soaked. It was 3am. My first thought was that the added pressure on my bladder caused me to relieve myself, as many pregnant women do. I rolled over on my side, made my way out of bed, and then it dawned on me....what if my water just broke? Not once did I ask for my husband's help or even call my doctor. I did what many modern day moms would have done; I Googled, "How to tell if your water broke." Confused by the information I read, I decided to catch a few additional winks of sleep until the doctor's office opened later that morning. After calling in, my OB/GYN advised me to come in right away. I was about 36-weeks pregnant with one prior c-section. The doctor examined me and discovered that my water had indeed broken. She instructed me to get to the hospital right away. Instead, I went home, combed my daughter's hair, made sure her clothes were out for the week, started cleaning her room trying to prepare for what would soon be a new world for us. At that time, the thought of having two children terrified me. My husband finally said, "Would you please just stop and let me help?"

As mothers, we feel like we have to do it all, alone. But the task and responsibilities in the home can be shared. Thankfully, my husband is always willing to help in whatever capacity necessary. But there have been times I truly wanted to ask for help, but I believe if it's in a person's heart to show support, they will do that willingly; without being prompted or begged. There are days when I literally work from dusk to dawn, because when I see a job that needs to be done, I want it done my way and right away. I suppose that's just the stubborn side of me. But as I get older, I realize that I am going to literally wear myself out if I continue this path. I'm not getting any younger, so I'm learning to delegate and assign my older children more responsibilities.

Mothers, there is no shame in asking for help, especially if you have family and friends who are willing. Seeking support does not make us weak, incapable, or vulnerable; it means you are wise. You recognize that even though you have the ability to do it all, you should never have to.

Mothers Never Stop Learning

I distinctly remember giving birth to my first child, just like it was yesterday. The unfamiliar labor pains awakened me out of a restless, uncomfortable sleep. Ten hours later, I laid eyes on this beautiful little girl with soft brown skin and eyes that resembled the night's sky. A single tear rolled down my face in awe at the miracle I'd been blessed with. My husband and I were overjoyed to begin this new phase of our lives. Only, we had truly no clue what we were getting into.

As the days continued, we experimented with various theories and parenting styles hoping to get the hang of it. I was pained at the sleepless nights and the difficulties of nursing and even what I now know to be signs of postpartum depression. My husband Roc and I were living in Virginia, at the time, and had no nearby family. We were both oblivious and naive and frightened that we would fail. Roc was so worried that he literally drove our daughter and me to Cleveland, where my parents reside. He drove back to Virginia to continue working. No, he wasn't trying to get rid of us. At least I don't believe that to be the case. We were just both so overwhelmed. I was afraid I was doing it all wrong, and he was afraid he couldn't help me. I stayed with my mom for several weeks and welcomed the extra support and confidence she was able to offer.

You see, parenting your first child is tough and, so far, it has not gotten any easier. I remember my oldest daughter, now almost 17, recently asked me how long it took to recover from my first pregnancy. My response, "I'm still working on it." By the time I thought I had a firm grasp on my parenting skills, our second miracle was born, and he required a completely different style of parental care. The cycle just continued with miracles three and four. They are all so different with various physical, emotional, mental, and psychological needs. I am forced to individualize motherhood to help them learn, grow and reach their full potential. The parenting style we use for my first-born son, Elijah, would be an epic failure for my youngest. If you raise your voice at him for any reason, it completely breaks his heart. My youngest daughter, Alonna, couldn't care less. She makes the corrections and keeps it moving. Elijah sets his own alarm to wake up at 5:30 in the morning, and Alonna would sleep all day, if we allowed her to.

From discipline to freedoms, to the way we communicate, it's essential to cater to the needs of each child. Even at my age, I still feel as if I'm learning and adapting. I never realized how difficult motherhood would be. As I dreamed of having children, I never considered that my parenting choices had to be calculated and intentional. Motherhood can never be mastered, only survived.

Sometimes You Just Have to Let Go

In just a short amount of time, my first-born will begin a new phase in her life. The culmination of her high school year brings about mixed emotions. I am absolutely, without-a-doubt terrified that this beautiful little girl, I once carried inside of me, will step foot into a world that shows no mercy. Will I be strong enough to control my plummeting emotions as I glare at the empty seat around our dinner table? The only certainty during this transition is that my heart and our home will no longer be the same.

Her laughter and strong sense of humor closely mirrors her dad's. I am far more reserved than she, yet her presence energizes my thoughts and actions. I dare not overlook the sound of her delicate singing voice; an echo so heavenly, even the angels pause to listen. I am certain the added silence in our household will, at times, be unnerving.

As she moves closer toward self-sufficiency, I can only pray that her faith and upbringing will guide her choices and behavior. We recently participated in a number of college tours in South Carolina. My most vivid memory is the container of condoms so neatly displayed in the dorm room entryway. Afraid my husband may die of an early heart attack, I perfectly positioned myself in front of the display. Only he notices everything. This is certainly not the most settling depiction of college life.

It seems like only yesterday I coached my baby girl into taking her first steps; sometimes falling and other times balancing like a pro. I know her strides into adulthood will be much of the same. She finally learned to walk when I decided to let go. Now I must gently release the grip I have become so accustomed to for the last 17 years. Sheltering her from every mistake would only be hindering her progress, though it's difficult to stand idly and watch. Mistakes are a part of developing wisdom and she, too, must create her own path.

My prayer is that the Lord will protect her and aid her in making wise choices. I have infused love, imparted knowledge, and attempted to demonstrate what it means to be a woman of character and morals. I did not always get it right, but perhaps she will also learn from the mistakes I made. Mother's work tirelessly for 18 years raising their children to become fully functional loving adults, but when the time comes, we panic. Instead, I will attempt to celebrate her soon-to-be self-sufficiency and consider that I no longer have to worry about someone rummaging through my closets and forgetting to return my borrowed clothes. There is a bright side to every story, right?

However painful this process, my emotions can no longer hold me hostage. Instead, I will celebrate her success and continue to offer support, as she needs it. As the days to her departure draw near, I will remind myself that motherhood is about preparing our children and releasing them to spread their wings. How will they ever soar to higher heights and deeper dimensions if we never allow them to leave the nest?

You Are Your Child's Biggest Advocate

As mothers, the love we share for our children is much deeper than we ever imagined. Before having children, I expected there would be a deep bond between my babies and me. I'd heard stories and read books about it. From the moment new life began growing on the inside of me, I felt an immediate connection. I did all I could to nurture and protect my children inside of me, because I knew that was my most significant responsibility at that time. No one else could feed and nourish my miracle. No one else could guard them against the possible dangers of lifting too much or eating the wrong foods. From the moment I nervously picked up the pregnancy test and laid eyes on those two blue lines, I immediately became their biggest advocate.

The years have passed, and my desire to protect and advocate for my children has only been strengthened. I doubt that will ever change. When my children started school, I was somewhat reluctant about speaking with teachers if I had concerns. I absolutely love educators and respect their tough position. But I always had to remind myself that I was my child's first advocate. If parents do not protect and stand up for their children, who will?

My older daughter attended first-grade at a private school not too far from our home. She was the only African-American child in her classroom. Honestly, I'm not sure that she even recognized that and I certainly was not going to point it out. It's in a child's nature to love and accept no matter what, so I refused to ruin that innocence. I picked her up from school one Friday. Before she stepped foot in the car, I immediately noticed that something was wrong. I could see the hurt in her eyes. As soon as she buckled up, my baby burst into tears. Mikayla explained how deeply embarrassed she was during a lesson about static electricity. The teacher placed a balloon over each child's hair showing how hair reacts to a negative static charge. As she went around the circle, everyone's hair stood straight up. In tears, my daughter explained that the teacher approached her last and proceeded to tell the class how this experiment may not work on her hair, because it was different from everyone else's. So she just stood there, and never had the opportunity to participate in that class activity. She was hurt. I was angry. I did not want my daughter to be singled out in class. I was not sure if I'd make things worse, for her, by bringing it up. I knew she still had about six months left in the year and I did not want to ruin anything for her. For one second I considered letting it slide, but I knew that if I (or my husband) did not stand up for my child, no one else would.

I've heard many mothers talk about turning into Mama Bear. When it comes to her cubs, mama bears have a vicious and protective nature; fighting until the very end to protect their cubs. So should we. I consider myself to be a pretty peaceful person but if you want to meet an unpleasant, unkind version of Cynthia, mess with one of my babies.

Now allow me to clarify, I am not one of those moms who believes her child is right 100% of the time. I refuse to stand up for my kid if they have been disobedient, disrespectful, or disingenuous. My children know that if they come to me complaining, they better have all of their facts correct. If I go to defend them and it turns out they're in the wrong, I will switch gears in the blink of an eye. Believe me, that has happened before! But if my children are being bullied, mistreated, or hurt in any way, Mama Bear is there with all paws on deck.

I will admit, I have learned to remain levelheaded when I find the need to defend my children. In most cases, the message is clearer and more defined when I express my concerns in a firm, but calm manner. As a mother, I will remain in my child's corner even after they become adults. I will stand up for them and defend them as long as they are doing what's right. As I tell them, they will always be my babies. Essentially, if you mess with my child, you mess with me. I know every mother reading this can relate!

No one will ever love our children the way that we do. They are the only ones who have ever heard the sound of our hearts from the inside of us. We should know our sons and daughters better than any teacher, any doctor, and any child-care provider. We know what makes them happy, what makes them angry, and what motives them to succeed. Never be ashamed for standing up for your child, especially when they are too young to stand up for themselves.

Quiet Mornings Lead to Better Days

I close my eyes and hear the gentle waves slowly beating against the sandy shore. I smell the aromatic fragrance of the salty sea and hear the spirited sound of seagulls. The sun's bright rays reflect upon the warm sand. I am calm, relaxed, and all is well in the world. What a tranquil, serene way to begin each morning. This is only my mental state of mind, not a physical location. But reflecting on calm and tranquil places helps counteract negative thoughts and stresses before the start of each day.

With four children, attending four different schools, our mornings are incredibly hectic. I know that once my feet hit the floor, it's non-stop from there. So even before I open my eyes, I try to begin my morning with thanksgiving, reflection, scripture, and meditation. Please don't tell my children, but sometimes when they knock on my door in the mornings, I lie quietly and pretend as if I'm asleep. I need just a few minutes to myself. It's somewhat of the calm before the storm. Once I open that door, everything breaks loose: finding lost book bags, packing lunches, fussing about clothes my children picked out...you know the routine!

My personality type is one that awakens ready to tackle a to-do-list. I have a difficult time relaxing once I get started, so taking a moment in the morning is vital for me. It sets the tone and rhythm for how I will react and handle challenges I face as the day progresses. When I first open my eyes, I always thank God for the opportunity to experience another day and I meditate on the many blessings I know I do not deserve. Positive thinking is key. As mothers, we have the tendency to exert mental and physical energy from the time we open our eyes until we lie down at night. It is vital to take a moment each morning to reflect upon your blessings, to meditate, and to focus. That peace will follow you throughout the day.

Speak the Truth Even if it Hurts

My three-year-old loves for me to watch him run. When I'm cooking, he walks up to me and says, "Mommy watch me go!" He puts one leg in front of the other, bends his knee getting into position and says with great excitement, "Ready, Steady, Go!" He takes off running through the dining room, makes his way into the living room and circles back into the kitchen. I stoop to his level, with a huge smile and energetically say, "Oh my goodness you are SUPER fast." Each time he smiles and in his mind, I'm quite certain he believes he is the fastest little fella to ever exist. Then he takes off to show me again.

I'm all for speaking positively into the lives of my children and encouraging them to always strive for more. I love to see their eyes light up when they know how proud we are of them. Research shows that words of affirmation greatly affect a child's mental and psychological development. But just as we speak affirming words, there are times when we must be candid, straightforward, and deliver news they would rather not hear.

As a mother, I have made a promise to always speak the truth to my children. It's not always enjoyable but I believe hearing the cold-hard facts are in their best interest. I want to build the type of trust with them where they realize they can come to me about any and everything and they will always receive a truthful answer, even when it doesn't feel so good.

My daughter is a great soccer player with hopes of making it to the Olympics, but she hates to practice. When she asks if I think she will become a famous player one day, I'm honest. "Yes, you are an awesome player with great potential, but you won't make it if you refuse to practice." She hates to hear that, but if I continuously tell her she's the best player on the team, without being honest about honing her soccer skills, I'm not being fair to her. We must find ways to encourage and boost our kid's confidence without setting them up to fail. I tell my children that they can do anything, but I also explain the hard work involved. Honesty is the best policy, even when it hurts.

We all want friends we can trust to tell us the truth, even if it's painful. Mothers, it's unfortunate, but the world does not care about our children. They will speak the truth in a way that will break their hearts. Whatever the situation, hearing the truth is easier coming from someone who truly cares about you. Speak the truth in a spirit of love. If we allow our children to leave home with false hope, we are setting them up for heartbreak and failure.

Say No To
"Because I Said So"

Children are curious beings. Mothers play a vital role in helping them understand how life works and how decisions are made. Growing up you may remember the oh-so-popular phrase, "Because I said so!" When you heard those four words that meant there would be no conversation or discussion. Simply, do as I say do. My parents used it religiously and so did most mothers and fathers of that generation. It was the norm and we survived. Parents knew they had your best interest at heart and in their minds, giving an explanation for their decisions was unnecessary.

If that well-known phrase, "Because I said so," still works well in your home, there will be no judgment from me. Occasionally, I still utter those words. It can be interpreted as; "Listen kid just trust me," or "I am the authority figure and you'll do as I say," or "I don't owe you a response," or "I just don't feel like answering right now." Take your choice! For me, "Because I said so" is a quick answer for a question I prefer not to answer in depth. But as a mother, I really have to determine if I am helping or hindering my child by answering with a short, empty response.

I want my children to have a solid understanding of choices and consequences. Understanding why and how you derived at the answer "no" helps children have a greater understanding about filtering facts before making a decision. "May I have cake?" "No, not today" "Why?" "Because you've had too much sugar already." Saying, "Because I said so" will not teach them that portion control is important. It does not teach them that moderation is important.

I understand that there are some situations that may not warrant a response to a child. It may involve subject matter they are not prepared to handle. But if I cannot explain it on their level, I'll simply respond with, "That's something I will discuss in more detail when you're a little older." Taking the time to help children understand choices helps break down barriers and creates a relationship built on trust. I feel no less of a parent, or authority figure, because I choose to explain my decisions to them. This does not undermine my influence. In fact, it places me in a position of power to educate, rather than take the easy route.

My children are social beings and love being in the company of family and friends. Sometimes they would ask to spend the night in homes of people I was not comfortable with. When they ask why I refuse to allow the sleepover they planned without my consent, I could easily say, "Because I said so." Instead, I take the time to explain the importance of getting to know a family before taking overnight trips. I've also explained how, sometimes, children are taken advantage of even in the homes of close family and friends. Saying, "Because I said so," robs them of an opportunity to learn and grow as individuals. They now understand my stance on sleepovers and rarely ask anymore.

Of course, I want my children to be obedient, even when they aren't given a reason. There are times I give them a demand they need to follow, without an explanation. But I am very selective with using that four-word phrase.

I try to take advantage of every opportunity possible to teach, so if they have a respectful question, I try to give a respectful answer. If they attempt to negotiate because they aren't satisfied with my response and think they know more, then all bets are off. My children know that I am not obligated to give them an answer, I chose to.

Never Give Up on Your Children

We would all love to believe that our children are perfect beings without fault. Wouldn't it be great if our sons and daughters adhered to every lesson we taught? We hope and pray that our children will one day change the world...or at least become productive citizens in society. The truth of the matter is, so many children grow up and make choices that break their parent's hearts. This is an unfortunate reality for so many mothers. They worked tirelessly to set a wonderful example of love and devotion, yet their children choose to go down the wrong path. Unfortunately, there is no fool proof method of raising kids. There are no guarantees that our children will be all we want them to be. Our job is to do the best we can to show love and support and our children then become responsible for the choices they make as adults. We cannot control that.

I've spoken with many broken-hearted mothers who have invested so much into the lives of their children. They aren't sure where they went wrong and most will blame themselves for the outcome of their child's life. Even mothers who more closely resemble perfection can raise children who refuse to do what's right.

I have a close acquaintance whose daughter is behind bars and serving a lengthy prison sentence. As a mom, I know her heart is literally torn into pieces. The pain and grief this must cause her is unimaginable. But I watch this devoted mother as she has full hope and faith that her child's life will one day turn around. Without even realizing it, this mother has impacted my life. She has taught me that no matter what our children go through we should love them unconditionally.

Our children will not always make positive choices but we can never give up on them. We must never lose hope. My kids are still pretty young and fortunately have not made any detrimental life-altering decisions. But no mother, regardless of how devoted, is exempt from that pain. Our job is to teach and mimic positive behavior. But we should not blame ourselves for every decision a child makes, especially when they are old enough to be held accountable for their own actions.

Almost every child will encounter periods in which they may become defiant and rebellious. My oldest daughter will tell you that during her middle school years she transformed into a creature from the great abyss. It seemed we butted heads over everything! Even when I thought she'd taken a turn for the worst, I loved her through it all and thankfully she returned to her senses. When you build a solid foundation at a young age, your love and an established relationship will help you endure those transitional phases.

The term, "unconditional love" is almost synonymous with motherhood. There is something about birthing and nurturing a child that will cause you to love, no matter the circumstances. Loving your children in no way means that you accept or condone their behavior. It means that you love without any strings attached. Love your children through every undesirable phase of their lives and simply be the best mother you can be. Encourage your children to live right, pray for them, love them, and no matter what, never ever give up on them.

Explore the Power of the Kitchen Table

The kitchen table is more than assorted pieces of lumber carefully constructed to display in a well-defined space within a home. Whether formal or informal, wood or glass, its main function is not to hold elegant décor changed with each passing season. The spills, the stains, the smudges, and smears all tell marvelous stories. If our wood-chipped dinner table could speak it would tell unforgettable tales of laughter, tears, love, arguments, discussions, debates, and card games. It would uncover secrets and reveal memorable meals shared with family and close friends.

If your table could talk, would it utter words of loneliness and solitude? Has the dust settled amid the properly placed, but rarely used cloth napkins and place mats? A kitchen table is the perfect gathering space for families to catch-up about the ups and downs of each day's events. It creates a sort of intimacy that cannot be gained upon cushioned couches that surround the family's big screen TV. The dinner table, though not quite as comfortable, positions you at the perfect eye level to share intimate glances with your spouse and look deeply into the eyes of your children; often revealing emotions they otherwise would never share.

There is something about the kitchen table that makes us feel like family. The crazy commotions and outbursts of laughter cause me to forget the craziness of my day. Hearing stories of friends and enemies, homework and exams, anxieties and reliefs all give me ideas of where my children stand in life and how I can best help.

Enjoying a meal without cell phones, and uninterrupted by the noise of a sitcom, allows me to have more in-depth conversations and communicate effectively with the ones I love most. It's a place where our children learn table manners, so as to not embarrass us while dining out. This assembled wood, in a fancy designed table, offers a significant reminder that the six people around this dinner table are on the same team.

Sure, the design of a dinner table is extremely crucial to the style of your home. Many spend weeks searching for the perfect style, size, and color to complement their kitchen cabinets or to match the freshly painted dining room walls. As you admire the craftsmanship of your round, rectangular, or oval-shaped décor, remember that a table is much more than a substantial piece of costly furniture. It is platforms and pillars constructed for the inspiration and elevation of the family; a centerpiece for celebrations and the perfect place for mealtime memories. Never underestimate your time around the table.

Block Out the Noise

As I write this short chapter, I can barely hear myself think. My oldest child is appallingly dancing while my youngest laughs hysterically. My first-born son is repeatedly calling my name. He is insisting that I watch the basketball game loudly playing in the background. My youngest daughter was just sent to bed for hitting her sibling, and now, my husband is singing the theme song to the movie Frozen. I am persistently trying to block out the noise. Someone, please rescue me.

The noise is tremendously loud and appears to completely surround me. It's difficult to focus my attention on this project but I've learned to manage. Over the years, I have become accustomed to the noise in my own home. This is the norm for us. But there are times, when the noise from the outside becomes more than I wish to bear. That noise I refer to is the nagging opinions and critique from others. You have enough children, you spoil them too much, let them cry it out, it's too early for them to date. Stop! Just stop!

When you become a mother, you will experience times when the noise approaches from every side. I could build a mountain with the advice I've been given. The opinions on how you should raise your family can truly become overwhelming. Although your friends and family members may have the best intentions, they can make raising a child even more difficult than it already is. The noise from others around you can be so loud that it will drown out your inner voice; a key element to raising your sons and daughters. Remember that those are your children, and no one knows them better than the woman who gave birth to them.

You can become so overcome by the advice and opinions of others, you will begin to doubt what you know in your heart is best. It's ok to simply say, "Thanks, but we have it under control," or you may need to separate yourself from those who feel the need to always meddle. No one should be allowed to impose his or her advice on you without your permission. It's true, that we should all be open to new ideas but when the unwanted opinions of others guide your decisions, you may be setting yourself up for a disaster. Just because an idea works for someone else's family, it may not go over well in your own home.

I still, occasionally, call my mother and seek her advice. I am familiar with her loving heart and her pure intentions. To me, her opinion matters and I consider any advice she suggests. But those who offer unsolicited recommendations often want to control your life or make you feel inadequate. Before you respond, consider the spirit in which those well-meaning words are given. If you feel uncomfortable or awkward with the opinions others try to force on you, just block out the noise momma and carry on. You know your children better than anyone.

Unconditional Love Makes the Difference

There is a four-letter word that will revolutionize the relationship you have with your children and create a solid foundation upon which to raise them. That word is love. Love is simple, yet its benefits yield powerful results. More than anything else in the world, children need to know that they are loved and valued.

Mothers are so often submerged in a sea of schedules, rigorous routines, and lingering lists of dreaded deadlines. It takes every ounce of energy just to survive a normal day's work, but in the midst of the hustle and bustle of motherhood, showing love is the most important of all.

It may be a gentle kiss on the cheek, spending quality time, or genuinely listening to problems that concern our children. Next to meeting basic needs, love is the second most essential part of a child's mental, physical, emotional, and social development. When children understand the depth of a mother's love, their chances of success and happiness are dramatically increased. They will be more confident and most likely have a positive perception of the world around them. Children who receive love find it much easier to express love.

It breaks my heart to know there are children who live with parents who never take time to even acknowledge their presence. I cannot wrap my mind around the fact that mothers and fathers knowingly abuse and neglect their sons and daughters. Every child deserves love; regardless of their race, gender, learning ability, or a parent's financial status. Sometimes, what we label as behavioral issues in children is simply a lack of love and attention.

There have been so many times I have failed to fulfill my mission as a mother. Frustrations in my own life have caused me to yell at my children when they didn't deserve it. I've buried my face in my cell phone instead of using that time to connect with my kids. We all have moments of motherhood we regret. But even in the midst of my mistakes, my children never doubt the love I have for them. During times I am obligated to discipline them for their mistakes, they still never doubt my love. Establishing a foundation of love causes everything else to fall in place.

I want my children to be successful. I want them to thrive spiritually, physically, mentally, and even financially. But more than anything else in the world, I want them to experience love. You may not have the funds to buy your children expensive gifts or take them on lavish vacations around the world. You may never give them the life you once dreamed of. But more importantly, do they know how much you love them? Do they feel wanted? Do they feel treasured? Do they feel like they are an integral part of your life?

The love you show is more precious than gold. Love is not in material gifts; it's in hugs, kisses and time spent. It's in notes, in calls, in words, and in deeds. It's in your compassion, your empathy, and in your patience. Love is unconditional and has no strings attached. Your love will affect every area of your child's existence and will impact their lives forever. You may never meet everyone's standards of motherhood but if you are guided by genuine love, there is no way you will fail.

Stay Strong♥

74819389R00073